Teen Money Skills

10 Secrets to Raise Your Financial IQ

Create Smart Money Habits

Earn * Budget * Save * Invest with Confidence

AI Applications to Accelerate Success

Freeman Publishing

Contents

Introduction

Did you know that only twenty-six states require high school students to take a personal finance course before graduating (Ramsey Solutions 2024a)? While that number is way up from recent years, it's still no wonder that many teens feel unprepared to handle their money effectively over the long term. As someone who struggled with financial literacy in my teenage years, I know firsthand how overwhelming and confusing money management can be. That's why I've made it my mission to empower teens like you with the knowledge and skills you need to take control of your financial future.

My goal with this book is to guide you through the most important money secrets that will raise your financial IQ. Together, we'll create smart money habits and learn how to earn, budget, save, and invest with confidence. I'll even show you how to use AI applications to accelerate your success. I aim to make financial concepts relatable and actionable for you.

This book is written for teens aged thirteen to nineteen but can help clarify money questions at any age. I believe that developing a positive financial mindset early on is important, and by breaking down complex topics into easy-to-understand terms, we're going to simplify the world of finance.. Whether you're just starting to think about money or you're already earning your own income with a part-time, or even a full-time job, this book has something valuable to offer.

Throughout the book, you'll find engaging activities, worksheets, and challenges that will help you apply what you learn to your own life. By actively participating in your financial education, you'll be setting yourself up for long-term success.

This book isn't just for teens, though. It is also designed to engage parents in the learning process. Working through the material together allows families to create a shared understanding of financial principles and a tradition of open communication about money. This collaborative approach is an important part of building a strong foundation for your financial future.

So, are you ready to take control of your financial destiny? Let's dive in and start building the money skills that will serve you for a lifetime. With dedication and the right mindset, you can achieve financial independence and success beyond your wildest dreams.

Chapter 1

Building the Foundation

Secret #1: Your dream, your options, your future life is determined based on the choices and decisions you make every day starting today.

It's a sad fact that only 24 percent of Millennials demonstrate basic financial literacy (National Endowment for Financial Education 2017). Though you're not a Millennial—as a teenager, you're squarely Gen Z—it's important to learn from the generations that came before you. That number is a staggering figure that shows how important it is to learn about money early on. I remember that when I was a teen, I had no plan for the money I earned beyond going to a movie or buying a new pair of shoes or piece of clothing. My money came and went with no clue and no plan—not to mention no idea that I was missing out on taking control of my future. That's why my goal is to help you build a solid foundation of financial knowledge so you can avoid making the same mistakes I did. It's important to develop a mindset that encourages smart money decisions and financial goals that guide your actions.

The Teen Financial Mindset: Growth - Think Big, Start Small

Your mindset plays a big role in how you handle money, and it's going to serve you well to absorb a growth mindset. A growth mindset means you're committing to being open to learning and improving, and it helps you see challenges as opportunities instead of obstacles. The original idea comes from the worlds of philosophy and education, but it fits perfectly with finance. If you think you can get better at managing money, you'll be more likely to try new things and learn from your mistakes. Financial educators like Carol Dweck emphasize the importance of mindset in achieving success. "The view you adopt for yourself profoundly affects the way you lead your life," she says (Dweck 2007). By adopting a growth mindset, you can completely change your financial habits and make smarter choices that ultimately benefit your future.

Starting small is key. You don't need to make big changes all at once; you can make a great start by saving a portion of what you earn or receive as allowance or gifts. It might be tempting to spend it; after all, you might think there's no possible way this can make a long-term difference. That's where you're wrong, as even a small amount saved regularly will add up over time. CHALLENGE: Get a jar or piggy bank and put a quarter in it every day. Every day, without fail, at least 25 cents. And no take-backsies. This money is untouchable. At the end of one year you will have nearly $100 and you didn't even miss that quarter you put away. To keep a mindful approach to handling the money you do have, you can set up a simple budget to track where your money goes, too. This doesn't have to be complicated; just list your income and expenses to see where your money is going and where you can cut back. Small, consistent actions build good habits that last, and over the long run, these habits help you achieve bigger financial goals.

Setting financial goals can also give you direction. Think about what you want to achieve, both short-term and long-term; maybe you want to save for a new phone or even a car. It's important to establish achievable goals and to break them down into smaller steps; this makes them less overwhelming and easier to tackle. It can be helpful to create a vision board with pictures and words that represent your goals. Do you have your dream car picked out? How about that electric guitar or a trip to Hawaii? Put a picture on your vision board and look at it every day. Write down the amount this dream costs on the picture. Do the math to figure out how much you can save each month and then how many months it will take to get you there.

Your mindset can help you make your dream a reality, and this visual reminder will keep you focused and motivated. When you set goals, you're more likely to make daily decisions that further what you really want to achieve. Remember, no matter how long it takes to make your dream come true, the time will eventually pass. When that time has gone by, you will have either made a consistent effort to make your dream happen or will have just let time pass without making the effort to achieve it.

> ***"If you really want to do something, you will find a way. If you don't, you'll find an excuse"***
>
> —**Jim Rohn**

It can also be a good idea to share your financial goals with your friends and family. You might find they're interested in similar things, and you can encourage each other to save toward your goals. You can also share financial books or resources. Discussing these topics helps you learn from each other and stay accountable. That's important, as when friends and family support your goals, you're more likely to stick to them.

Set Your First Financial Goal

Secret #2: Start early and be consistent.

If your question is "when should I start saving for my retirement", the answer is "Yesterday" so there's no time to waste. Take a moment to think about something you want to save for. It could be big or small; all that matters is that it's a goal for you to reach. Now, break it into smaller steps: How much do you need to save each week or month? Most importantly, where will the money come from? Even thirteen and fourteen-year-olds can earn extra money with a little imagination and a helpful attitude. Check out these examples and come up with a list that fits your own options:

- Lawn mowing or weeding flower beds
- Raking leaves
- Shoveling snow
- Babysitting
- House Sitting
- Pet care
- Dog walking
- Grocery shopping or running errands
- Selling old toys, books, or clothes online
- Washing or vacuuming cars

Babysitting, in particular, can be a great gig. Parents of small children would welcome a helper who can run around the park with toddlers and younger kids with lots of energy. Also, let go of any notions of it being "a girl's job"—whether you're a boy or a girl, you can kick a soccer ball around, climb the playground equipment, dig in the sandbox, and generally supervise very active small children. Being kind and attentive to active little ones will make you very popular with parents. Even playing in their own backyard lets parents have a few moments to do their own chores, make phone calls, or pay bills while the little ones have fun playtime.

I was doing this when I was thirteen, and I was in high demand. In the summertime, with pool parties, birthday parties, or any other big get-together, it's always helpful to have an extra pair of eyes and hands to keep up with the kids. I even took lifeguard training and a CPR course. Later, I became the night-time babysitter for couples to have a date night, playing a board game with the kids before bedtime and then doing my homework. You wouldn't believe how much money I earned on New Year's Eve alone.

Whatever route you take, though, create a simple plan for earning and saving your money and share it with a friend or family member who can support you. Keep track of your progress and celebrate when you reach your goal. This exercise helps you practice setting and achieving financial goals, laying the groundwork for future success.

Demystifying Money: Simple Terms for Complex Concepts

Secret #3: The best way to prepare yourself financially is to actively plan on INCREASING YOUR EARNING POWER year after year and INVESTING your savings wisely so it grows for you.

Money can seem complicated, but it doesn't have to be. Let's break down some key terms. Budgeting is making a plan for how you expect to spend your money (more on this in Chapter 3). Saving, meanwhile, is exactly what it sounds like: keeping some money aside for special purchases or unexpected future needs. Investing, meanwhile, is when you use your money to try and make more money.

Remember, prices go up yearly on essentials like food, rent, insurance, clothes, entertainment, etc., based on inflation and other factors. If you're planning on buying the same things every year, you have only two choices: earning more money or reducing your expenses. It's difficult to find lower-cost food, rent, insurance, clothes, or entertainment, so you may sometimes have to give up the things you want. Not recognizing this fact is the reason that, according to Bankrate, 57 percent of American workers think they are behind where they should be on their retirement savings (Christian and Strickland 2024). While there are always going to be factors beyond your control, putting off your ability to retire and having to work far later in life can sometimes be the result of poor planning in your early years.

Saving money is kind of like charging your phone. You don't let your phone's battery die completely before charging it; instead, you top it up regularly. The same goes for saving, where you add a little to your savings whenever you can. When you have enough money to pay your bills on time, you build good credit. Don't worry about that for now; we'll get into it in detail in Chapter 5. There are also concepts like compound interest, which we'll talk about in Chapter 7. The important thing is to get started making what money you can now in order to be prepared for the future. Curiosity is your best friend when learning about money, so don't hesitate to ask questions when it doesn't seem to make sense. Keeping curious is how you grow your understanding and confidence in handling money.

Financial Stories: Learning from Teen Successes

What if you could start a business while you were still in high school? It might sound impossible, but many teens have actually done it with remarkable success. Take the story of Sara 'Saray Young, an Atlanta-area entrepreneur who began selling homemade jewelry under her brand SaraSaray. Young not only sold her jewelry online but actually started writing about it on a blog with tips for young girls and women—particularly plus-sized women who, in Young's words, "may not have realized their value and worth." This led her to invites for events, workshops, and even teaching classes, ultimately growing her name recognition and her brand even more (Shoutout Atlanta 2023). Sara 'Saray Young's story is a great example of following your values and ultimately finding commercial success.

Another story is that of Memphis native Moziah Bridges. Bridges discovered at a young age that he couldn't find bowties he liked—so he started making his own. Bridges started small, sewing his bowties by hand under the brand name Mo's Bows. Eventually, his brand grew to the point where major retailers carry Bridges' products, his company produces bowties for all thirty NBA teams, and he's sold more than $700,000 worth of handmade dress accessories—all while still a teenager (Lodge 2024).

Stories of successful teen entrepreneurs come from people with different backgrounds, too. Some grow up in communities where money is tight, while others might have more resources. Each story reflects a unique approach to money management, and each is that of someone who blazed their own trail. What they have in common is that their entrepreneurial paths highlight the need for careful budgeting and planning. Without a clear understanding of costs and profits, even the best ideas can fail. Your savings journey ties directly into your ability to set goals for yourself. By knowing what you want and planning how to get there, you give yourself a far greater chance of success. These principles are not just for adults; they can guide teens like you in making informed decisions every day.

Hypothetical Case Study: Teen Investor Success

Let's say there's a teen named Elena who decides to invest in the stock market. She opened an account on Robinhood.com and starts with small amounts, using money she saves from babysitting. Researching companies and understanding market trends, meanwhile, allows her to make informed choices. Her investment grows, teaching her how patience and research can pay off, and eventually, she's making far more money than she ever put in. This experience shows Elena the power of investing, a lesson she continues to apply for years later.

Elena's story is a reminder that anyone can learn about investing, regardless of age or background. With the right approach, even small investments can lead to significant returns over time. If you're under the age of eighteen, an adult can open a custodial account for you at a brokerage firm like Charles Schwab,

Fidelity, or E*Trade. Most companies don't have a minimum investment required to open these accounts; you just need an adult who will help you put your money to work (Segal 2024).

Meanwhile, if you're over eighteen, you can open an online trading account at SoFi Invest, Ally Invest, Fidelity, Public.com as well as Robinhood.com. You can even buy fractional shares of stocks and exchange-traded funds (ETFs). You can go with single stocks of well-known companies like Amazon, Apple, Netflix, and Microsoft, or you can read about the basics of investing and see if you prefer funds that bundle these together for you (Chen 2024a). You can also access other options like Total Market Index Funds, which automatically diversify your investments across entire industries (Blokhin 2024). Some stocks pay dividends, while others just get bigger and more valuable. If any of these terms don't sound familiar, like "what's an ETF"? just Google it or do a search using any of the currently exploding internet AI search engines or check out stockanalysis.com.

Overcoming Financial Fears: Confidence Starts Here

Many teens feel anxious about money, and that's totally normal. It's common to worry about not having enough money or making mistakes with it, particularly if your family has a history of bad spending or money management habits like mine did. These fears can be paralyzing, and you might feel completely unsure of how to start managing your finances. Remember, though, that every expert was once a beginner.

Fear of not having enough money often stems from not knowing where your money goes. You might see your friends spending freely and wonder if you should, too. On the other hand, without a clear picture of where your money is going, it's just as easy to baselessly worry about running out. The key here is to make sure you keep track of your finances so you're always in the know and you are making mindful choices.

Anxiety about making financial mistakes can come from all sorts of places; what if you choose the wrong bank account or spend too much on something you don't need? These worries can make you hesitate to take any financial steps. While this is understandable, you shouldn't let fear hold you back. As mentioned I earlier, start small with low risk and build your way up. Financial confidence comes from taking action one step at a time.

A supportive environment makes a big difference. Find people you trust to give you advice on money; this could be a parent, a teacher, or even a friend who's good with saving. If you find the right person or people to give you advice, you don't have to do this alone. Financial mentors can offer guidance and share their own experiences, helping you avoid common pitfalls and make better decisions. There are also many resources available to help you learn about financial literacy. Books, podcasts, and online courses can offer valuable tips, so explore them. Those financial terms and buzzwords aren't so intimidating once you understand the basics (and we'll go through a lot of the big terms in detail anyway in later chapters). The more you learn, the more confident you'll become.

Resilience and adaptability are key skills in money management. Everyone makes mistakes, and that's okay. What actually matters is how you recover from them. Let's say you spend too much on a new gadget and regret it later. Instead of dwelling on it, think about what you can do differently next time. Maybe you can set a spending limit or decide you'll wait a week before making any big purchases. The best plan for teens is to learn from financial mistakes—even theoretical ones—while the stakes are still low.

Exercises that practice financial problem-solving can help build these skills, so try creating hypothetical scenarios where you face a financial setback. Think about possible solutions and how you would handle them. This sort of practice prepares you for real-life challenges.

It's important to remember that money management is a skill you develop over time rather than something you're born with. Nobody gets everything right on the first try, and that's perfectly normal. The key is to keep learning and adapting. Each step you take builds your financial confidence; as you become more comfortable with managing your money, you'll feel more empowered to make bigger decisions about your future. Financial literacy doesn't mean simply looking at numbers but fully understanding your relationship with money and learning how to make it work for you.

The Power of Goal Setting: Mapping Your Financial Future

Secret #4: Create a comprehensive financial plan with clear goals.

Setting financial goals means intentionally plotting a map for your future. It gives direction and purpose to your actions. Without clear goals, it's easy to wander aimlessly—and then wind up wondering where your money went. You wouldn't wake up one morning and decide you're just going to drive from the East Coast to California with no plan, would you? You might get there eventually, but you'd definitely waste a lot of time and money along the way.

Planning your financial future is much the same, and goals are a great way to help yourself focus. They remind you why you're saving instead of spending. Short-term goals are great for keeping you motivated. Saving for a concert ticket is a good example of a short-term goal; it's both rewarding and quickly attainable. Long-term goals, like saving for college, require more pre-planning and patience—but they have the added benefit of teaching you discipline and perseverance. Having both types of goals means you always have something to work toward, no matter how distant.

You will need a real plan to achieve these goals. Start by writing down what you want. Be specific; instead of writing "I want to save money," jot down "I want to save $200 by the end of the year." Break it into smaller, more manageable steps from there, using worksheets to outline the specifics of each step. This organization will eventually help you see your progress. Decide when you want to achieve each step, as a timeline keeps you accountable and creates a sense of urgency. Goals without deadlines are just dreams, and by building a detailed plan, you turn your goals into tangible targets. Make this sign and put it on your vision board to keep you heading in the right direction.

> ***"If you really want to do something, you will find a way. If you don't, you'll find an excuse"***
>
> —**Jim Rohn**

Visualization can help you stay focused, too. Your vision board should be specific with images and words that represent both your short and long-term goals. Place it where you can see it daily. This constant reminder will keep your goals at the top of your mind. **Journaling** can be another powerful tool. Write about your progress and look for what works and what doesn't. This will help you learn and adapt, and it also provides motivation when you see how far you've come. Visualization and journaling work hand in hand to keep your goals alive and growing.

Accountability is likewise important. Share your goals with someone you trust; this could be a friend, family member, or mentor. Whoever you pick, this person will become your accountability partner. Don't worry that they might be judgmental or critical if you don't succeed at every step; find the right person who will both support you and keep you on track. Set regular check-ins to review your progress and keep yourself focused. Always be willing to adjust your plan if needed; remember, flexibility is fundamental. As life changes, so should your goals.

Finances probably seem like a big and scary deal right now. That's ok; you're allowed to feel a bit overwhelmed by them. Just know that over the following chapters, My aim is to give you every detail you need to feel fully prepared for your financial future. Take a deep breath, and let's get started.

Chapter 2

Earning and Entrepreneurial Skills

Have you ever considered that what you love doing in your free time could actually earn you money? Many teens haven't yet realized that their hobbies can be more than just fun activities; they can become profitable, fully monetized ventures. You could turn your passion for photography into a business that pays for your new camera or use your crafting skills to make products that others want to buy. Hobbies like these can open doors to financial independence, and I aim to show you how to turn them into successful side hustles.

Side Hustle Success: Turning Hobbies into Income

The first step in turning a hobby into a side hustle as a teenager is to identify what you're truly passionate about. Do you spend hours drawing, creating digital art, or making your own jewelry? These interests could be the foundation of a business. For instance, teen sisters Caroline and Isabel Bercaw took their love for making bath bombs and turned it into Da Bomb Bath Fizzers, a company that now sells over 500,000 bath bombs each month (Sternlicht 2020). Their story shows that what starts as a fun activity can grow into something much bigger as long as you're willing to put in the time and effort.

Once you have a hobby in mind, it's time to think about how to market it. Setting up an online store is a great way to reach customers beyond your local area, and platforms like Etsy or even your own website can help showcase your creations. You'll need to think about pricing, which can be tricky. It's a good idea to research similar products and see what others are charging, then think about your costs and time. Don't undervalue your work, but you want to keep your prices competitive. Marketing your products is just as important as creating them, too. Use social media to share your story; engaging photos and posts can attract a lot of potential customers. Building a brand around your hobby can do a lot to make it more appealing and trustworthy. Do a search for the selling platform that would work best for your particular business like Amazon Handmade, Big Cartel, Folksy or Bonanza.

Balancing school, hobbies, and a side hustle can feel overwhelming, but with a bit of organization, it is possible. It can be helpful to create a schedule that includes time for schoolwork, your side hustle, and relaxation time. Set realistic goals and prioritize tasks by importance and deadline; you want to make sure that you're not neglecting your schoolwork even as you pursue your new business. You want to work smarter, not harder, as balance is an important part of avoiding burnout and keeping your passion alive.

Success stories of teens who have managed side hustles can offer valuable lessons. Hillary Yip, founder of MinorMynas, started her project to help kids learn languages through video sharing at ten years old. Her path wasn't without challenges; she had to balance her schoolwork with running the platform and working through various technical issues. But she persevered, learning from each setback and eventually becoming the youngest CEO in the world (Rose 2023). Her story shows the importance of persistence and adaptability.

Launching Your Side Hustle

Thinking about things you love to do; what makes it unique? Write down your ideas for turning it into a side hustle. Outline a simple plan that includes your goals, potential customers, and how you'll market your work. Set a small, achievable target for your first month. Let's say you like photography. Put the word out in your circle of friends and family that you're available for kid's birthday parties and special events. Come up with a basic hourly rate for your time and a price for either digital copies of the pictures chosen or hard copies if they want pictures they can frame. Share your plan with a friend or family member for feedback on the details. This will help you take your first step toward making your hobby a source of income.

Digital Natives: Leveraging AI and Online Platforms for Profit

As we move deeper into the Information Age, making money online is more accessible than ever before. Platforms like Etsy, YouTube, and Fiverr have opened up new opportunities for teens to earn using their skills and creativity. Is your passion scouring resale shops for hidden gems? Etsy is perfect for selling handmade or vintage items. It's a place where your custom art, handmade art and crafts, or unique products can find their audience. YouTube, meanwhile, allows you to share videos on topics you're passionate about—gaming, tutorials, history, you name it—and with enough viewers, you can earn money through ads and sponsorships. Make a YouTube video about how you do your thing, like create your own jewelry and point viewers to your selling platform. Fiverr is a gig worker platform where you can offer services like video production, graphic design, or writing for a fee. Each of these platforms has its own set of rules and audience, but they all offer a chance to turn your talents into profits.

To get more familiar with the explosion of AI enhanced side hustle opportunities check out Basic Generative AI: Beginner's Guide to Artificial Intelligence Available on Amazon.com. Check it out at www.amazon.com/dp/1963333209

You can download a free eBook version with Kindle Unlimited or get the paperback version. This is a **link** to the Amazon page or scan the QR code to find it.

Building a strong online presence with positive reviews is an important part of attracting customers and clients. It's a lot like your digital storefront; you want something bright and flashy enough to attract people walking (browsing) by. Start by creating a compelling digital portfolio that showcases your work or services. Use high-quality images and clear descriptions to highlight what makes you unique. Keep your portfolio updated with your latest work, and be sure to engage with your audience by responding to comments and messages in a timely manner. This interaction builds trust and shows that you care about your customers. As such, social media is a powerful tool to promote your portfolio and reach a wider audience, so share your work on platforms like Instagram, TikTok, or Facebook. TikTok Shop is quickly becoming one of the most viral platforms to introduce new products.Use hashtags and tag relevant accounts to increase your visibility. Consistency is key, so post regularly, even daily, and keep your content fresh and engaging.

You should also make it a point to share interesting content that relates to your products or services, such as behind-the-scenes looks, tutorials, or customer testimonials. Encourage your followers to share your posts to reach new audiences. Another important aspect is search engine optimization (SEO). This involves using the right keywords in your content to make it easier for people to find you through search engines, so it's important to learn about creating content that ranks well in search results (Melinn 2024). These skills might seem challenging at first, but they go a long way toward helping you stand out in an increasingly crowded online marketplace.

While the digital world offers great opportunities, it also comes with responsibilities. Maintaining both your digital safety and your ethical standards is important. Always protect your personal information by using strong, unique passwords for your accounts —and enable two-factor authentication whenever possible. Be cautious about the information you share online; avoid giving out sensitive details like your home address or phone number. Ethical business practices are equally important; always be honest about your products or services and treat your customers fairly. Deliver what you promise and handle any disputes professionally. Building a reputation for integrity will, over the long run, earn you loyal customers who trust your brand.

Building Your Digital Portfolio

Start a project by selecting one platform to showcase your skills or products.

- Develop a profile that includes your best work, clear descriptions, and engaging visuals.
- Set a goal to post new content weekly.
- Track your interactions and note what types of content get the most engagement.
- Adjust your strategy based on what you learn.

Even if your first business doesn't take off, the experience of building a digital portfolio will help you understand what works best for online businesses going forward.

Teenpreneur Toolkit: Important Skills for Young Entrepreneurs

Secret #5: Every obstacle and challenge is a valuable opportunity—a chance to learn, adapt, and grow stronger.

Starting your own business might seem scary, but it's simpler than you'd think as long as you can master a few fundamental skills. One of the most important of these is basic accounting and financial management. You need to understand where your money is coming from and where it's going; this means keeping track of your earnings, expenses, and profits. You can use simple spreadsheets or accounting apps to organize this information—and you're definitely going to want to have it organized, as knowing these numbers helps you make informed decisions and avoid running into financial trouble. It's like having a map that shows you where your business stands at any moment.

Customer service and sales techniques are also extremely important. Treating customers well matters both because they are the backbone of any business and because positive reviews from satisfied customers will help you grow your customer base. A happy customer is likely to return—and might even bring friends with them.

Learn how to communicate clearly, listen to what your customers need, and always aim to solve problems quickly and with a smile. Sales skills help you present your product in the best light, so make sure you understand what makes your product unique and be ready to explain its benefits. You can practice these skills by role-playing different scenarios with a friend where you act as the customer and ask the tough questions you would expect any other service provider to know. This prepares you for real interactions while building your confidence.

Creativity and innovation drive successful businesses and keep you ahead of the curve. It's always a good idea to brainstorm ideas regularly, so set aside time each week to think about how you can improve your product or service. Check out your competition; what are they doing that you can do better? It's also a good idea to look at businesses led by young people—including the ones we've already talked about—for inspiration.

It's also important to understand that innovation doesn't necessarily mean creating something entirely new; sometimes, it just means improving on what's already there. Ralph Waldo Emerson once said—in different words, but with the same sentiment—"Build a better mousetrap, and the world will beat a path to your door" (NMAH 2011). This means when you create a superior product or service, buyers will more likely come to you. Of course, they also have to know about the product first, so put as much effort into promoting and marketing your ideas as you do into creating them.

Having a solid business plan is another important step. A business plan outlines your goals and how you plan to achieve them, and it includes details about your product, target market, and financial projections. Use templates to guide you through writing your plan, starting with a simple draft and refining it as your business idea develops. Again, look at examples of successful plans from other young entrepreneurs to see how they organized their ideas; learning from those who came before you is always a great idea. A clear plan should both guide you and attract potential investors or partners, showing that you're serious about your venture and you've thought it through.

Check out AI powered business planning solutions for small businesses and startups like Upmetrics and Lavender.ai among others.

Adaptability is a trait every entrepreneur needs. Business will have ups and downs—that's inevitable—and it's how you handle them that matters. Learn from those who faced challenges and adapted prior to achieving success. Michael Dell, for instance, founded Dell Computers in his college dorm room with $1,000 at age nineteen and faced intense competition. He adapted by focusing on direct sales and customer needs—a choice that set him apart from many of his competitors (The Editors of Encyclopedia Britannica 2025).

Adaptability means being open to change and having a willingness to adjust your plans as needed. If you're not there yet, even younger teens and pre-teens can recognize what they're working and saving toward. When that opportunity arrives, they'll be ready to tackle a new venture head-on.

Drafting Your Business Plan

If you think you're at the stage where you can start a side business or monetize your hobby, start by taking a long, hard look at your business idea. What problem does it solve? Who are your customers? Assuming you can come up with satisfactory answers to these questions, outline your goals for the next year. Use a template to organize your thoughts, and include sections on marketing and finances. Share your draft with someone you trust for feedback so you can get another pair of eyes on it. This will help you think through your business idea and prepare you for the next steps.

Earning with Purpose: Matching Your Values with Ventures

Do you want to build a business that doesn't only make money but also makes a difference in the world? Value-driven businesses aim to do just that. They match what they stand for with how they operate. For some, this might mean focusing on sustainability, like using eco-friendly materials or reducing waste. Others, meanwhile, might prioritize social impact by supporting local communities or donating a portion of their profits to charity. Maya's Ideas, founded by Maya Penn, sells eco-friendly accessories and donates part of the profits to environmental causes (Klein n.d.). Businesses like these are designed to find success while bringing a sense of fulfillment to their founders. When your work reflects what you believe in, it becomes a core part of who you are.

Of course, you'll first need to understand your personal values if you want to start a value-driven business. What matters most to you? Is it protecting the environment, helping others, promoting fairness and equality, or something else entirely? Take some time to really think about these questions and write down what comes to mind. Once you know your core values, think about how they can shape your business. If you're passionate about sustainability, it could be a good idea to always use recycled materials in your products. If education is important to you, a portion of your sales could support local schools. Making and selling friendship bracelets in school colors and donating to special school projects gives you a wide customer base. Matching your business with your values enables you to build something that can really inspire both you and your customers.

Balancing profit with purpose might seem challenging; after all, businesses need to make money to survive. But it's definitely possible to do both. Some companies integrate social responsibility into their business models. This can mean different things: fair pay for workers, sourcing materials from ethical suppliers, recycling as much of their materials as possible, etc. Doing this allows them to support their values while attracting customers who share those values. Successful social enterprises show that you don't always have to choose between making a profit and making a difference. A business can thrive while also contributing positively to society.

Community involvement plays a big role in running a value-driven business. Engaging with your local community can provide support and strengthen your network, so think about starting a project that benefits your neighbors, such as organizing a cleanup event or hosting a workshop. Earth Day is celebrated on April 22nd every year, and many groups organize cleaning and beautification programs in local communities.

Collaborating with local organizations can also amplify your impact. Networking with like-minded individuals and groups can open up new opportunities, as it allows you to share resources and ideas. This collective effort can lead to greater success for everyone involved. There's also the added benefit that being active in your community helps build trust and credibility for your business.

If you want to seek more national opportunities to connect with others in a socially responsible way, there are also organizations that do just that. Rotary is a great example; they're a huge network of more than 45,000 clubs that collaborate to deal with various social issues. With options ranging from providing basic needs to protecting the environment to fighting disease, there's likely something in their portfolio that appeals to you (Rotary n.d.).

Networking for Teens: Building Connections That Count

Networking might sound like it's only for adults or big business professionals, but it plays a huge role in both personal and professional growth for teens, too. Having a network of mentors and friends who support you and share their knowledge is not a strength to be underestimated. Connecting with the right people can open doors to new opportunities you might not find on your own. A mentor can guide you, offering advice based on their own experiences, while peers in your field can provide support and collaboration. A young entrepreneur might meet a tech mogul who helps bring their app idea to life by funding it or other young tech experts who can think of ways to make it better. Connections like these can greatly improve both your learning and your career path.

Building a network starts with simple steps. Local events or workshops can be a great place to meet people with similar interests.

Heck, even a school club or community group can offer networking opportunities. The key is to look for events that spark your passions. Don't forget about social media; platforms like LinkedIn and even Instagram can connect you with industry professionals. Follow people who inspire you and engage with their content; a thoughtful comment on a post can lead to a life-changing conversation. Remember always that networking doesn't mean taking advantage of others but building genuine relationships that benefit everyone involved.

Strong communication skills are another big key to effective networking. Being able to start and maintain meaningful conversations can set you apart, so practice active listening, which means really paying attention when someone else is speaking. When you communicate, be clear and concise. Ask open-ended questions that encourage dialogue; this shows you're interested and engaged. Non-verbal cues like eye contact and nodding can also make a big difference, so practice these skills in everyday interactions to become more comfortable. Role-playing scenarios with friends, meanwhile, can be a fun way to improve both verbal and non-verbal communication.

Building a strong network takes time and effort. If you're willing to put in both, though, it can lead to an extremely supportive community that helps you thrive. Pay it forward, too; networking's advantage is not simply what you can gain but how you can help others. Building these relationships creates a network that supports your dreams and ambitions. As you continue to explore and expand these connections, remember that each person you meet can teach you something new—and with each lesson, you grow closer to achieving your goals.

Check out options through local Chambers of Commerce or Rotary Clubs to see if organizations like The Interact Clubs have a local program in your area to mentor and guide young people looking to develop leadership skills. Kiwanis International has Key Clubs that focus on leadership development. Lions Clubs, Civitan International, and Optimist International also have youth programs or clubs that focus on service and leadership development. Having an experienced mentor can give you the necessary support and guidance to achieve success in all aspects of financial development.

Chapter 3

Smart Budgeting Techniques

So you've received your allowance or paycheck from your part-time job, and you feel flush with cash. Before you know it, though, it's gone, your bank account is as barren as a desert. Where the heck did all the money go?

If you've ever experienced this, you're not alone. Many teens—and let's be honest, many adults—face this challenge because they don't have a plan for their money. Remember when I mentioned budgeting back in Chapter 1? This is where we're really going to get into it. As a reminder, a budget is a written plan that helps you decide how to use your money wisely. It's designed to help you balance your spending with your savings so you don't end up broke before your next allowance or paycheck. You've heard the term "living paycheck to paycheck"? Too many people end up in this situation.

Budgeting lays the foundation for financial independence by helping you learn to live within your means. When you budget, you track your income and expenses to make sure you don't spend more than you earn. This skill becomes even more important as you get older and take on more financial responsibilities. By learning to budget now, you prepare for the future when you'll need to manage your own money, pay bills, and save for things like college or a car.

How to Make a Budget

So, how do you create a budget? You have to start by listing all your sources of income. This could include your allowance, part-time job earnings, or even money you receive as gifts. The next step is to list all your expenses. Think about everything you spend money on, from snacks and clothes to phone bills and gas. Now, break these expenses down into two categories: needs and wants. Needs are essentials like food or transportation; they are things you need in order to function or survive. Wants, on the other hand, are non-essential items like a new video game or concert tickets; they are things that might make life worth living but which aren't themselves. This helps you see where your money is going and identify areas where you can cut back if needed.

Let's look at a sample budget an adult might have as a starting point:

INCOME:

- Wages (Take-Home): $5,000
- Interests/Dividends: $400
- Miscellaneous: $250

Total: $5,650

EXPENSES (Needs):

- Car Payment/Insurance: $400
- Rent: $1200
- Utilities: $300
- Groceries: $600
- Child Care: $1,500

Total: $4,000

Subtracting the expenses from the revenue here leaves you with $1,650 after all primary expenses—not that much when you take into account that everything listed in Expenses is a "need" rather than a "want." That $1,650 doesn't include anything for Savings and has to cover all of your entertainment desires and other Wants for the month, not to mention things like going to a restaurant once in a while. Regardless of the specifics, you could easily use a similar template to create your own budget, replacing adult costs such as "Rent" with expenses you might currently have as a teenager.

One common budgeting mistake is overestimating income. You might think you'll earn more than you actually do, which can lead to overspending. The sample budget above calculates $5,000 in take-home pay, but you would need to be making in the $70,000 per year range for this to be possible, considering payroll deductions as well as state and federal taxes. As a result, it's important that you be realistic about how much money you have coming in. Another pitfall is ignoring small, frequent expenses. Those daily coffees or snacks might not seem like much, but they add up quickly. Being mindful of potential costs like these allows you to avoid financial stress and stay on track with your budget.

Reviewing your budget regularly is important, too. When your income and expenses change, your budget should also reflect that. Set a habit to review your budget at least every month—more often if you keep finding yourself running out of money mid-month. This is also a good time to see if you're meeting your goals; if not, adjust your plan. Use a simple checklist to assess your budget. Are you spending too much on wants? Do you need to save more for future needs and expenses? Questions like these help you stay focused and adapt to any changes in your financial situation.

Monthly Budget Review Checklist

To help with your budget review, use the following checklist:

1. List all income sources and review monthly for changes.
2. Review all expenses and categorize them as needs or wants.
3. Calculate the total spent on each category.
4. Set a realistic goal for savings.
5. Identify areas where you can save or need to adjust.
6. Set goals for the next month based on your assessment.

Using this checklist can make your budget review process simpler and more effective, keeping you organized and getting the most out of your money. Budgeting might seem complicated at first, but with practice, it will become second nature. As you get more comfortable with budgeting, you'll also find it easier to make decisions that line up with your financial goals. Ultimately, budgeting isn't intended to restrict you but to make sure you can enjoy your money now while also saving for future opportunities.

You've heard about people who, as soon as they get any money at all, it's "burning a hole in their pocket". That means they are in the habit of spending every cent as soon as they get it. This habit leaves you with a pocket full of holes and nothing to show for your efforts. Don't be one of those people, it's immature at best and creates a long term problem at worst.

Tech-Savvy Budgeting: Apps and Tools for Every Teen

Luckily, you don't have to do all your budget tracking by hand with a notebook and a pen. In recent decades, budgeting apps have become extremely important tools for managing money, offering a convenient way to track spending and save for the future. Many of these are geared toward younger customers, too. Highly rated apps like Rocket Money, You Need a Budget (YNAB), and Lunch Money sometimes have a free version as well as a subscription version.

Other apps like Acorn, Greenlight and PocketSmith are popular choices among teens. Rocket Money helps you see all your accounts in one place, making it easier to track where your money goes. YNAB encourages you to give every dollar a job (meaning you assign every last dollar to a specific expense), helping you prioritize spending. Lunch Money packs a lot of useful budgeting data into a few easy-to-read and navigate pages. Each app has unique features tailored to different needs, and exploring these options can help you find the right fit for your lifestyle.

Choosing the right budgeting app involves thinking about what you want to achieve. Some apps focus on saving, while others emphasize more clever ways of spending. Features that match your financial goals are always a good idea. If you want to save more, find an app that sets savings goals and tracks progress. For those who struggle with overspending, choose an app that sends alerts when you approach your spending limit. App interfaces matter, too; some people prefer a simple design, while others like detailed graphs, so you should figure out which works for you. Read reviews and try a few options to see which feels best; you might discover that the right app takes the stress out of managing your money.

Integrating technology into your budgeting routine can simplify the process significantly. Set up alerts and reminders to help you stay within your limits; these notifications can prevent you from overspending. Many apps offer features like automatic categorization of expenses, too, which can save a lot of time. You can also use spreadsheets for a manual approach if you want. While this can be a bit more work, it also gives you more control over how you record transactions. Creating a spreadsheet with columns for income, expenses, and savings can provide a clear overview of your finances, allowing you to see patterns and make adjustments as needed.

The benefits of digital tracking are numerous. Technology provides information about your spending habits that you might not otherwise even notice until you see it visualized through charts and graphs. You might suddenly realize you're spending more on eating out than expected, which can guide you toward making smarter choices. By seeing how small changes affect your budget, you can make informed decisions about cutting back or reallocating funds. Digital tools thus offer a level of detail and accuracy that's hard to achieve with pen and paper.

Flex vs. Save: Dealing with Peer Pressure and Spending

Peer pressure can sneak into your finances without you even realizing it. Think about the last time your friends suggested going out for pizza or buying the latest gadget; you might have felt that tiny nudge to join in even if your wallet didn't agree. It's normal to want to fit in and do what everyone else is doing—but this can lead you to spend money you don't really have. If all your friends are planning a weekend trip, you might feel stuck between joining them and sticking to your budget. Recognizing peer pressure is the first step in overcoming it. Ask yourself, "Am I spending because I want to or because I feel I have to?" This question can help you pause and think before making a choice that might negatively affect your finances. Remember, every choice has a consequence.

Finding the right balance between spending and saving is a delicate balance. You want to enjoy life and have fun, but you also need to think about your future. One good way to do this is by allocating a portion of your income for fun activities. Decide on a set amount you can comfortably spend each month on things like movies, games, or eating out. This way, you get to enjoy yourself without feeling guilty as long as you don't go over your budget. At the same time, set limits on discretionary spending by keeping track of non-essential expenses. If you notice you're spending too much on things you don't really need—or even necessarily want—it's a sign to cut back. By maintaining this balance, you can have the best of both worlds, enjoying the present while securing your future.

Mindful spending requires both planning and self-control. Creating a wish list is a good place to start. Write down things you want to buy, whether it's a new pair of sneakers or new electronics, then prioritize them by importance. This helps you focus on what truly matters and avoid impulse purchases. Another tactic is the twenty-four-hour rule. If you feel the urge to make a significant purchase on a whim, wait a day before pulling the trigger. This gives you time to think about whether you really need it. A lot of the time, you'll find that the initial purchasing excitement fades, and you can allocate that money for something that's more important to you. By making mindful spending decisions, you take control of your finances instead of letting your impulses control you. It's better to have a pocket full of money than a pocket full of holes.

Talking about money with friends can seem awkward, but it doesn't have to be. Open discussions about financial goals and challenges can create a supportive environment. You might be surprised to find that your friends share similar concerns, in which case it's a good idea to suggest budget-friendly shared activities. Instead of going to an expensive concert, plan a group movie night at home. You can also encourage your group to set financial goals together by carefully saving for a trip or a big purchase. Working toward these goals as a group allows you to hold each other accountable and motivate one another. This turns financial conversations into something positive and empowering.

Dealing with the pull of peer pressure while managing your finances isn't always easy, but it's possible with some awareness and planning. Ultimately, your financial choices are yours to make, as are the resulting consequences. By recognizing peer pressure, finding balance, and talking openly with friends, you create a path to financial independence that's both enjoyable and sustainable.

The 50/30/20 Rule: Simplified Budgeting for Teens

Budgeting can sometimes feel like a puzzle with too many pieces—but the 50/30/20 rule can simplify it and make money management a lot easier for teens. This rule divides your income into three categories: Needs, Wants, and Savings (or debt repayment). The idea is to spend no more than 50 percent of your income on Needs; these are things you can't live without, like food, shelter, and transportation. Next, 30 percent is available for Wants; these are extras like going to the movies or buying new clothes. Finally, at least 20 percent should go into Savings, which is money you set aside for future needs or emergencies. This method is straightforward and helps you see where your money should go (Ayoola n.d.).

You will need to know your monthly income and expenses to make use of the 50/30/20 rule. Calculate how much money you receive each month; as a teenager, this is likely from a part-time job, allowance or gifts. Write down all your expenses and see which ones are Needs and which are Wants. Once you have this information, you can allocate your money accordingly. If your income averages $300 a month, $150 should go to Needs, $90 to Wants, and $60 to Savings. Granted, you're probably not going to have as many Needs as a teen, but this step-by-step approach still makes it easy to see how the rule applies to your life and helps you stick to a plan.

Sometimes, life doesn't fit into neat categories. Your income might change from month to month, or you might have special circumstances. Maybe you get more hours at work during the summer, or you have to buy school supplies at the start of the year. Luckily, the 50/30/20 rule is flexible, allowing you to adjust based on your needs. If your income increases, you might save more than 20 percent. If you have a big expense, you might need to spend more on Needs for a while. The key is to adapt the rule to fit your unique situation without losing sight of your financial goals. Structured budgeting, like the 50/30/20 rule, brings clarity to your finances, simplifying decision-making by providing a clear guide on how to spend and save your money. You don't have to guess where your money should go; instead, you just follow the rule and make adjustments as needed. This structure also helps build a habit of regular savings, as setting aside money each month creates a safety net for unexpected expenses or future plans. Over time, this habit strengthens your financial stability and prepares you for bigger and bigger financial responsibilities. Never, ever let unnecessary Wants steal from Savings and you will have a winning plan.

Key Takeaway

The best part is that the simplicity of the 50/30/20 rule makes it easy to understand and follow. It's a tool that empowers you to take control of your money without overwhelming you with complicated calculations. Using this rule will help you make smarter financial choices and keep you focused on what's important, giving you confidence in your ability to manage your money and work toward your goals. This approach lays a solid foundation for financial independence and encourages you to think about the future—without abandoning your enjoyment of the present.

Real-Time Adjustments: Adapting Your Budget on the Go

Life is full of surprises, and clearly, your budget needs to keep up with them. You might plan your month perfectly only to find out there's a school trip you didn't account for. On the other hand, you might suddenly be presented with the opportunity to pick up extra shifts at your job during the holidays, giving you increased income. These changes in income and expenses mean your budget has to be flexible to help you avoid stress while still meeting your goals. Your budget is a living thing that needs to grow and change as your life does. Whether it's unexpected school events or seasonal shifts in your job, adapting your budget keeps you in control.

Learning to adjust your budget in real-time is a valuable skill that gets stronger the more you do it. One good way to exercise this muscle is to track any changes in your income or upcoming expenses as soon as they happen. Got a birthday gift or an extra paycheck? Write it down. Did you have to buy a birthday gift for someone else or supplies for a last-minute project? Add that, too. You want to make sure you're always staying aware of what's going in and out of your wallet. Creating a buffer category in your budget can help. Basically, this is a small amount of money set aside for unexpected items. If you don't use it, it rolls over to the next month, building a cushion for the next surprise. Having a buffer keeps you prepared without throwing off your entire budget or dipping into your savings.

You'll also want to be proactive with your finances and take charge before problems arise. Set alerts on your phone or budgeting app to warn you if you're nearing your spending limit; this gives you time to cut back or adjust before you find yourself in a bind. Regular check-ins are also extremely important, so take a moment each week to look at your budget. Are you on track, or do you need to make changes? The more you engage with your budget, the more confident you'll feel in managing it.

Real-time adjustments turn your budget into a powerful tool, allowing you to handle life's unpredictability with ease. Staying flexible and proactive keeps financial surprises from derailing your plans. As you become more comfortable with adjusting your budget, you'll build skills that will serve you well not just during your teen years but throughout your adult life.

Chapter 4

Saving Strategies

Let's say you're in your early twenties, and you're planning a special trip with friends. It wasn't easy, but you've saved up enough money to enjoy the adventure without worrying about the cost. That sounds great, but it is probably impossible, right?

Not so; this dream can become a reality if you start saving now. The real goal of saving money isn't setting aside cash for a rainy day but building a future where you can afford the things you want without stress. The earlier you start saving, the more you can benefit from compound interest, which allows your money to grow over time. By saving even a small amount now, you set yourself up for financial security later.

Getting Started with Saving

The biggest question is: How do you begin this savings process? It starts with the idea of "paying yourself first." This means setting aside a portion of your income as soon as you receive it; you should treat it like a bill you have to pay every month. Doing this prioritizes saving over spending on things you don't need and helps you build a cushion of savings for the future. As time goes on, the money you've built up will grow thanks to compound interest. In a nutshell, compound interest is when the interest you earn on your savings starts earning interest itself; it's a snowball effect that makes your savings grow faster the longer you leave them untouched. There's a reason Albert Einstein once said, "Compound interest is the eighth wonder of the world. He who understands it, earns it. He who doesn't, pays it" (Downie 2024).

You should also think about creating "saving buckets" to organize your savings more efficiently. These are categories for different goals, such as short-term, long-term, and emergency savings. Short-term savings might be for fairly inexpensive things you want soon, while long-term savings could be for expensive electronics, college, or a car. Emergency savings, meanwhile, are for unexpected expenses like a broken phone or a surprise school fee. Visualizing your savings with a pie chart can help you see where your money will be going; this allows you to make sure you're saving enough in each bucket to meet your goals. Put this Savings Pie Chart on your vision board so you're reminded of why giving up that after-school latte means you'll eventually get something even better.

Saving money has psychological benefits, too. Having savings can reduce stress and give you peace of mind, as you don't have to worry about how you'll pay for unexpected expenses when you have a financial cushion. This security can, in turn, make you feel more in control of your life. Saving money can be an empowering feeling, especially for teens. Knowing you have money set aside can help you feel more independent and confident in your ability to handle life's challenges.

Financial psychologists often talk about the emotional impact of saving and say that saving money can improve your relationships and overall well-being. This makes sense, as when you're not stressed about money, you're more likely to have positive interactions with others. You can focus on enjoying life rather than worrying about finances. Starting to save now helps you develop healthy financial habits that will benefit you throughout your life.

Saving Challenges: Gamifying Your Savings Goals

Saving money can usually feel like a chore, but what if it could be fun and exciting? Gamification means adding game-like elements to tasks that aren't usually games and allows you to do just that. This makes saving feel like an adventure rather than a dull slog. Turning your savings goals into a game where you earn rewards for reaching milestones boosts your motivation to save more and stick to your goals. Some apps even let you build virtual cities or earn points as you save, which makes the process even more engaging. Check out apps like Savings Spree, FamZoo, Greenlight and Acorns Early.

You might have heard of the "52-Week Savings Challenge," a popular way to save money over a year by saving a little more each week. You start with $1 in the first week, $2 in the second, and so on; by the end of the year, you'll have saved a significant amount without feeling the pinch (Little 2024). Another fun challenge is the monthly no-spend challenge, which is as simple as picking a month and trying not to spend money on anything unnecessary (Ramsey Solutions 2024b). This is a great way to save money and rethink your spending habits. Both challenges offer a structured yet flexible approach to saving. Turning saving into a game can help you develop habits that last.

Getting your friends involved can make saving even more fun. Forming social savings groups is a great way to support each other; you can even set up a savings club with your friends where everyone has a common goal. Sharing progress and tips in a group chat keeps everyone accountable, and you can encourage each other and celebrate when any one of you reaches your goal. This social aspect adds a layer of fun to saving, turning a solo task into a team effort. Working together allows you to strengthen your commitment to saving.

Tracking your savings progress can do a lot to help you stay motivated. Let's say you want to use a visual savings tracker—like a savings thermometer. You color in sections as you reach different savings levels, making the colors go up over time. This helps because seeing your progress visually can be more satisfying than just looking at numbers, giving you a sense of accomplishment each time you fill in a new section. Setting up regular check-ins with yourself or your savings group can also help. Whatever method you pick, recognizing your progress keeps you focused on your goals and encourages you to keep going.

Gamifying savings turns a task that might otherwise be boring into something much more exciting and rewarding. It can fundamentally change the way you think about money and make saving a positive experience. Incorporating rewards, challenges, and social support allows you to build a strong savings habit. It's an approach which helps you achieve your financial goals while making the process a lot more enjoyable.

High-Interest Accounts: Maximizing Your Savings Potential

High-interest savings accounts, in concept, are simple: They're a special place for your money where it grows faster than in a regular account. High-interest accounts are designed to give you a better return on your savings by paying a higher interest rate compared to standard accounts. They mostly work like regular savings accounts but offer better growth due to the increased interest rate paid. The difference is that a regular account only gives you a small percentage of interest, while a high-interest account can offer much more. This means your money works harder for you, and over time, it can make a significant difference in how much you save (Burnette 2024).

When choosing a high-interest savings account, it's important to compare different options. Look at the interest rates first; a higher rate means more money in your account over time. Don't forget to check for fees either, though. Some accounts might charge for things like maintenance or withdrawals, but you want an account that offers a high rate with low or no fees. Accessibility is another key factor. You want to be sure you can easily deposit and withdraw your money when needed, but some high-interest accounts have minimum opening balances or limit how often you can access your funds. Think about what features matter most to you, like online banking or automatic transfers, and be sure to take your time to research and find an account that fits your needs.

Interest can dramatically increase your savings. To see how, let's do a simple calculation. Let's say you have $1,000 in a high-interest account with a 5 percent annual rate. At the end of the year, you earn $50 in interest. If you leave this interest in the account, the next year, you earn interest on $1,050. This is compound interest in action; it means you earn interest on your initial deposit and also on the interest it has already earned. We'll get into this deeper in Chapter 7, but for now, just know that over several years, leaving money alone and letting it grow can lead to significant growth.

Emergency Funds: Preparing for Life's Unexpected Turns

Secret #6: Build and maintain a healthy emergency fund.

Life can be unpredictable, and sometimes you'll just be going about your day when something unexpected and deeply unfortunate happens. Maybe you break a tooth and need urgent dental care. Maybe your bike gets stolen, and you need to replace it fast. Situations like these tend to come out of nowhere, and they can be very stressful—especially if you don't have money set aside for emergencies. This is where your emergency fund comes in handy as a financial cushion that helps you manage unexpected expenses without throwing your budget totally off course. Having this safety net means you won't have to borrow money or dip into your savings for other goals.

But how much should you save for an emergency fund? For teens, having $500 to $1,000 is a good start. This amount can cover most small emergencies and give you significant peace of mind. It's important to remember, though, that your emergency fund is not for everyday spending. Instead, it's reserved for true emergencies like medical bills or urgent repairs. Maybe you don't need to spend it on those emergencies right now—in all likelihood, your parents or guardians will cover them. But one day, you will, and you're going to want to have money ready. Building this fund starts with setting a monthly contribution goal. Decide how much you can set aside each month; even if it's just a small amount, it still adds up over time. Automatic transfers can make this easier by moving money into your emergency fund without you even having to think about it.

One of the biggest challenges with an emergency fund is not using it for non-emergencies. It can be tempting to dip into it for things that aren't urgent. Maybe there's a sale on something you've wanted for a while, or your friends are planning a weekend getaway. But using your emergency fund for these things defeats its entire purpose. A good way to resist this temptation is to keep your emergency fund in a separate account; this way, the money doesn't mix with your regular spending money. You can even choose an account that isn't linked to your main checking account, which makes it even harder to access on impulse.

The benefits of having an emergency fund, meanwhile, are pretty clear: Having money when you really need it does a ton to reduce your overall stress levels. Financial advisors often stress the importance of emergency savings, saying it provides both financial security and emotional peace. Knowing you can handle unexpected costs without scrambling for cash can be extremely empowering.

Building an emergency fund might not seem exciting, but it's one of the smartest financial moves you can make for the long term. It prepares you for life's surprises, giving you stability and confidence. As you continue to grow your financial knowledge, remember that an emergency fund is a key part of a solid financial plan.

Chapter 5

Understanding and Managing Credit

So you're ready to rent your first apartment or secure your dream job, but there's a catch: They want to check your credit. Surprised? You're not alone; many teens don't realize how important credit is until they need it. Credit is basically financial trust. It's a way for lenders to decide whether you are likely to pay them back. It's also a much more recent creation than you might think, as credit scores were only first created in 1989 (Paul 2024). But while Baby Boomers and those before them never had to deal with every present credit scores, unfortunately, it's now here to stay for every generation that came after them—and Generation Z is no different.

Good credit opens doors to many opportunities; it helps you rent an apartment, open a bank account, get a car loan at a reasonable interest rate, or even buy a cellphone plan. Establishing strong credit early can smooth the path to these milestones and more, while making mistakes with your credit can haunt you for years, if not decades. Understanding credit now, while you're still young, can do a lot to set you up for future success.

What Even Is Credit?

Credit consists of several key elements. At its core, credit is an agreement where you borrow money and promise to pay it back later. The idea is that good credit history shows lenders you can handle money responsibly. Credit reports play an important role in this process as they maintain detailed records of your financial history. They show how much debt you have, your payment history, and whether you've been reliable in the past. These reports come from three major credit bureaus: Equifax, Experian, and TransUnion. Each bureau collects and reports your financial activities to anyone considering providing you with loans or services. This includes financial institutions (for a mortgage or credit card), lenders (for a car loan or student loan), and retailers (cell phone companies, landlords, furniture, electronics, utility companies). One important thing to note: You can access your credit report for free once a year from AnnualCreditReport.com. It's a very good idea to do so, too, in order to review your report for accuracy of your name, address, and list of current credit cards or loans. You always want to make sure someone else's debt hasn't been added to your credit report by mistake and to watch out for identity theft (Kagan 2024).

Building credit might seem like an overwhelming hill to climb, especially if you're just starting out—but there are ways to get a head start. One effective method is becoming an authorized user on a parent's credit card, which means your name is added to their account. This allows you to benefit from their good payment history without being responsible for the bill. It's a simple step that can positively impact your credit history. Of course, if your parents don't have good credit, this might not be a good idea. Another option is a secured credit card, which requires a cash deposit as collateral. This can teach you to manage credit responsibly and build your credit history over time. Both strategies can provide a foundation for developing good credit habits.

The advantages of maintaining good credit extend far beyond just buying things. When you have a strong credit history, lenders see you as less risky, which typically leads to lower interest rates on loans. You can save thousands of dollars over the life of a car loan or mortgage because of a good credit score. Good credit also simplifies approval processes. Whether you're applying for an apartment or a job, many landlords and employers strongly take your credit history into account, viewing it as a measure of your reliability and responsibility. Having good credit greatly increases your chances of securing these opportunities.

Start Building Your Credit

1. Talk to your parents about being added as an authorized user on their credit card. Discuss how this can help your credit history. If necessary, you can keep that credit card in a drawer and only use it with permission.
2. Research secured credit cards suitable for teens. Compare the requirements and benefits.
3. Check your credit report for free once a year using AnnualCreditReport.com. Always make sure all information is accurate and up-to-date.

Taking these steps early on allows you to begin to build a strong credit foundation before you ever actually need it. This foundation is an extremely good idea for securing long-term financial independence and achieving your future goals.

The Credit Score Game: How to Play and Win

Credit scores might seem like an incomprehensible mystery, but they play a big role in your financial life. A FICO credit score—again, that thing we've only had for thirty-six years—is a number that purports to show how good you are with money assigning a range that usually sits between 300 and 850. Lenders use this number to decide whether they should lend you money. A higher score means you're seen as less risky, which makes it easier to get loans or credit cards with the lowest interest rates. With a lower score, though, you might find it hard to borrow money, and lenders might charge you higher interest rates because they see you as a bigger risk. Understanding your score can help you make better money choices.

Several factors affect your credit score, and one of the most important is your payment history. This is pretty simple: Paying your bills on time shows lenders you are reliable, while late payments can hurt your score. This isn't the only factor, though; another one is credit utilization, which is how much of your credit limit you're using. If you have a credit card with a $1,000 limit and you use only $300, your utilization is 30 percent. Keeping this number low is good for your score. Consistently using more than 30 percent of your available credit can have a negative effect on your FICO number. The length of your credit history also matters. Generally speaking, the longer you have had credit, the better, as it shows lenders you have experience managing money.

Improving a low credit score takes time and effort. Paying all your bills on time is one of the best ways to keep your score up, so set reminders or automate payments to help you stay on track. Keeping credit card balances low is another smart move, so try not to use more than 30 percent of your credit limit. If you can, make every effort to pay off your balance in full each month, as this shows you can manage your credit well and you're not wasting money paying interest. Avoid opening too many new accounts at once, too, as each application can lower your score by a few points for a short time. Be patient and focus on building good habits over time; always keep in mind that building exceptional credit is a long-term project. Recovering from bad credit takes even longer.

It's also important to check in with the credit monitoring companies regularly. This helps you catch mistakes on your credit report —mistakes that can badly hurt your score if not promptly corrected. You can use free credit score services to keep an eye on your score and send you alerts. Some banks even have your FICO score on your account page on their app. Be sure to check your full credit report at least once a year and look for errors like wrong account information or incorrect balances. If you find a mistake, contact the credit bureau to fix it. Staying on top of your credit report helps protect your financial health, which is important, as when you apply for student loans or large purchases, you don't want there to be any surprises.

Credit scores might seem like just a number, but they have a big impact on your life and can eventually save you thousands of dollars in interest payments. Understanding how they work and taking steps to improve your score sets you up for financial success.

Examining Your Credit Score Plan

Think about your current financial habits. Are there areas where you could improve? Write down two or three actions you can take to boost your credit score. These could include setting up automatic payments, paying the statement balance in full every month, or reducing your credit card balances. Review your plan every few months to track your progress and make changes as needed. You want to play the credit score game to win, and regularly checking in on your score is a good way to do it.

Credit Cards Uncovered: Smart Use and Common Pitfalls

Credit cards might seem like magical pieces of plastic that let you buy things for free, but that's a trap. In fact, there's more to credit cards than meets the eye, and understanding how they work can save you from a lot of trouble down the road. A credit card allows you to borrow money—up to a certain limit—to pay for things. You have to eventually pay this money back, though—ideally every month to avoid paying extra in interest. This borrowed money is different from a debit card, which simply takes the money directly from your bank account at the time of the purchase. Using a credit card wisely can actually help build your credit score, as it shows lenders that you can handle borrowed money responsibly. Every time you make a purchase and pay it off, it influences your credit score for the better.

There are numerous advantages to using credit cards responsibly. The biggest and most obvious is helping you establish a positive credit history as long as you make payments on time. As we've talked about, this history can make it easier for you to get loans or other lines of credit later on. That's not the only benefit, though; credit cards can also offer rewards or cashback, depending on the card you choose. This means you can earn points for every dollar you spend, which can be redeemed for things like travel or shopping vouchers. Some cards also offer protection on purchases, extending warranties, or offering refunds if something goes wrong. These benefits can add real value to your everyday spending if you use them wisely.

However, credit cards come with their own set of challenges. One of the biggest pitfalls is overspending; it's easy to lose track of how much you've spent when you're not using cash or watching your bank account balance. If you spend more than you can pay back, you'll start accruing high-interest credit card debt, which means you'll owe a lot more money than you originally borrowed. Obviously, this will make it a lot harder to pay off your balance.

Missing payments is another problem; if you don't pay at least the minimum amount due each month, you'll start to incur late fees. These fees can add up quickly, making it even harder to clear your debt. Missed payments can also negatively impact your credit score, which makes it harder to get credit in the future. Staying on top of your credit may seem like a hassle, but believe me when I say it's much harder and takes a lot longer to repair your credit than to proactively manage it in the first place. Having a credit card isn't a license to spend freely; it's a test of your creditworthiness and financial maturity. Being aware of these risks and actively avoiding them can save you from significant financial headaches down the road.

Managing a credit card effectively does require some planning and discipline. One practical tip is to set up automatic payments. Doing so means you'll never miss a payment (as long as there's money in your bank account, anyway) and helps you avoid late fees. Automating the process removes the risk of forgetting and the stress of remembering due dates. Some credit cards also come with annual fees you need to pay to maintain an account; it's wise to choose a card without an annual fee, especially if you're just starting out. Make an effort to find cards that offer the best perks for your lifestyle, whether it's cashback on groceries or points for travel; that way, you can make the most out of every purchase.

Much of good credit card management comes down to self-control. It's easy to swipe your card without thinking, but those small purchases can add up. While I've rarely had to question charges listed on my credit card statement, a year or so ago, I ran into a major issue. I found dozens of charges from $12 to $50 for fast food restaurants for phoned-in food orders—meaning they never actually saw a card but simply took down the credit card info manually. This meant someone had gotten a hold of my credit card number and made numerous unauthorized charges. I called the customer service number on my credit card and explained the issue. The customer service agent could tell that my past practices had never included fast food restaurants—not to mention that the charges for that particular month didn't match my normal charging patterns. I also had a history of paying my account in full every month and generally had a high credit score. The fraudulent charges were ultimately removed from my account and referred to their fraud department for investigation.

I never use a credit card for small purchases at locations that I don't consider secure. If you make purchases online, try not to enter your credit card information into various websites. Instead, use highly rated payment services like PayPal, Apple Pay, Wise, or Payoneer for better protection of your credit information. Try not to carry a balance from month to month, either. Paying your balance in full whenever you can helps you avoid interest charges and keeps your credit score healthy. If you do need to carry a balance, make sure it's manageable and that you have a plan to pay it off quickly.

Using a credit card can be a smart financial move if you understand how to manage it—but it does require responsibility and awareness of the potential risks. Following these tips will help you build a strong credit history while taking advantage of the benefits credit cards can offer.

Avoiding Debt Traps: Strategies for Staying Debt-Free

Secret #7: Living within your means is a habit that can protect you from debt.

Debt is not to be taken lightly, and it can build up a lot faster than you realize. You might start with a simple purchase or a small loan, but if you don't manage it well, that smaller amount can quickly spiral out of control. One of the biggest dangers of debt is high interest rates. Remember when we talked about high-interest savings accounts? This is kind of like that—only it doesn't benefit you at all. Sometimes, you can borrow only a small amount but have to pay back much more money because of the interest you're being charged. This is how debt grows, and it's a big cause of the trillion-dollar student loan crisis in the US (Ziv 2025). Each month, interest adds up, which makes it harder to pay off the original amount. Over time, this can lead to a cycle of borrowing more just to cover the interest and not even touching the main debt. Picture paying a monthly amount for decades only to never see your total balance actually drop; this is a reality for many people, and it's why it's important to understand how interest works and choose loans or credit wisely.

Debt can also bring a lot of emotional stress with it. Worrying about how to make the next payment or how much you owe can weigh heavily on your mind, affecting other parts of your life like school, work, or relationships. After all, it's hard to focus on your goals when you're constantly worried about money you don't have to pay off old debts. This is why keeping debt in check before it becomes overwhelming is so consequential to so many areas of your life. Knowing how to manage debt can prevent this stress and make your financial life much more manageable.

Debt is a slippery slope that can be very hard to overcome, and careful budgeting, as we talked about in Chapter 3, can make a huge difference. Spending within your means helps you avoid unnecessary debt and also allows you to save for emergencies, avoiding the need to borrow when unexpected expenses arise. Avoiding unnecessary loans or credit card debt is also important. Before taking on debt, ask yourself if it's truly necessary and if you can pay it back quickly without straining your finances.

To be able to grow your retirement wealth, consider that any high-interest debt, like credit cards, should be paid off as soon as possible. Continuing to carry high-interest debt will eat into your investment returns. Once your high-interest debt is paid off, build up your emergency savings account so you won't need to make expensive withdrawals from retirement accounts.If your employer offers a 401(k), set up recurring automatic contributions from your paycheck so you never see that money. If your employer has a matching program, even better. That's free money to grow your retirement savings much faster. When changing jobs, be sure to take your retirement account with you. If your employer doesn't have a retirement savings plan, you can open an IRA or solo 401 (k) on your own through a broker like Charles Schwab or Fidelity.

Even with the best planning, debt can sometimes become hard to manage. This is where debt consolidation can come into play. Debt consolidation means combining multiple debts into a single payment. Having one payment to think about each month can make it a lot easier to manage your debt (particularly psychologically). It might also lower your interest rate and save you money in the long run. However, be careful because consolidating debt doesn't erase it, and you'll still need to pay it off. Make sure to understand the terms to guarantee it's a good fit for your situation, as otherwise, you risk falling farther behind and even deeper into debt.

Debt can negatively impact your quality of life, but with the right strategies, you can avoid it. By budgeting carefully, living within your means, and planning for emergencies, you can stay debt-free and focus on your goals.

Chapter 6

Introduction to Investing

It's time to dive deep into a subject we've touched on a bit: investing. Basically, investing means buying things like stocks, properties, or other financial assets with the hope that they will increase in value over time. When it's successful, investing allows you to grow your money while you sleep. It's a way to put your savings to work for you. The goal is to earn more money than you put in—this growth is known as "return on investment" (ROI). Over time, these returns can help you build wealth and achieve your financial goals. Many people think investing is only for adults with lots of money, but that's not true. Teens can start investing, too, even though it's likely to involve smaller amounts.

Getting Started Small

Starting small with investments is a smart strategy, especially for teenagers. You don't need a lot of money to begin; thanks to technology, you can invest with as little as a few dollars of starting capital. Apps like Greenlight and Stockpile allow you to buy fractional shares of stocks. This means you can own a piece of a stock even if you can't afford the price of a whole share. If a single share costs $100, for instance, you could invest $10 and own one-tenth of that share. This approach makes investing accessible to everyone, as you can start with amounts as low as $5 or $10 and gradually increase your investment as you become more financially comfortable. These apps also offer educational tools to help you learn about investing as you go. Before you commit to one investing app in particular, it's a good idea to compare a number of them for things like fees and how they fit with your overall investing vision (such as it is).

Patience is big when it comes to investing. Unlike short-term trading, which involves buying and selling quickly to profit from market changes, long-term investing focuses on holding investments for years through up cycles and down, to allow your money to grow through the power of compounding, which we talked about in Chapter 4. Historical examples show that long-term investing can be very successful. Look at the stock market; it's had its ups and downs, but over the long haul, it has generally increased in value. You can buy dividend stocks like PepsiCo (PEP) or Chevron (CVX) that pay you a share of their earnings periodically or you may prefer growth stocks like Amazon.com (AMZN), Alphabet (GOOGL), Meta/Facebook (META) or Chipotle Mexican Grill (CMG) that are reasonably priced and expected to go much higher in the future as the companies involved grow. Staying patient and not reacting to short-term market changes is extremely important; don't jump in and out of stocks like you would with day trading. Instead, buy highly rated dividend and growth stocks for the long-term and ignore the periodic drops in the market—unless you take advantage of "buying the dip" in picking up extra shares when the price temporarily goes down.

Dealing with the world of investing does require the right educational resources. Luckily, there are a lot of books, websites, and courses that can teach you the basics. A great book to start with is *The Little Book of Common Sense Investing* by John C. Bogle, founder and former CEO of the Vanguard Group. It explains investing in simple terms and emphasizes the importance of low-cost, long-term strategies (Bogle 2007). Online platforms, meanwhile, sometimes offer free courses that cover everything from the basics to more advanced topics. Websites like Investopedia are great for articles and tutorials that break down complex concepts into easy-to-understand language. Exploring these resources enables you to build a strong foundation and make informed decisions about your investments.

Creating Your Investment Plan

Think about what you want to achieve with your investments. Is it saving for college or buying a car? Write down your goals and the timeline for each. Research an investment app that allows fractional shares like Stockpile or Greenlight. Start with a small amount—as little as $10—and choose a stock or fund that interests you. Track your investment and watch how it grows over time. This is a low-cost way to help you understand the basics of investing and set you on the path to financial growth.

Stocks, Bonds, and Beyond: Your Investment Options

Investing offers a variety of paths, and each has its own potential benefits and risks. Stocks, bonds, real estate, and commodities are among the primary options available to investors. Stocks represent shares of ownership in a company; when you buy a stock, you become a part-owner of that company. If the company does well, the value of your stock likely rises, potentially resulting in a profit if you sell the stock at a higher price than you initially paid for it. One wrinkle to be aware of is that you will owe income tax on any profits made in the stock market.

Bonds, on the other hand, are like loans you give to companies or governments. In return, they promise to pay you back with interest over time. Bonds can provide a steady income and are less volatile than stocks, but they usually offer lower returns in comparison (Davis 2025). Real estate, meanwhile, involves buying property like houses or land. It can be a solid investment if property values increase, but it does require more money to invest upfront—property isn't cheap, after all. There are also commodities, such as natural resources like gold or oil. The downside to these is that their prices can be unpredictable, often changing daily or even hourly due to market conditions.

Each of these options has unique characteristics that make them suitable for different goals and desired risk levels. Stocks can offer high returns, which makes them attractive to many investors. When a company grows or becomes more profitable, its stock price often goes up, which means your investment can potentially grow quickly. Stocks, however, are also known for their volatility, as prices can rise and fall sharply in short periods for reasons having nothing to do with the company itself. Changes in the Fed rate of interest, inflation, geopolitical uncertainty and even weather can affect a company's stock price. This unpredictability makes investing in stocks somewhat risky if you aren't in it for the long haul. Bonds are usually more stable, as they offer fixed interest payments, which can provide a reliable income. With municipal bond ratings ranging anywhere from AAA to D, you can get some level of comfort in the safety of your investment. Investment-grade bonds would typically be BBB- or higher. The returns from bonds are generally lower, though, meaning they might not keep up with inflation over time.

Understanding these pros and cons helps you decide which investments match up best with your financial goals and risk tolerance. For the time being, as you learn about investing and increase the size of your investment portfolio, it might be best to concentrate on stocks and stock funds that pay you dividends or offer long-term growth potential.

Researching investment options is an important step before committing your money. Look at company performance if you're interested in stocks—things like revenue, profit, cash position and growth potential. Market trends can also provide information about how stocks might perform in the future. For bonds, meanwhile, understanding credit ratings is important. These ratings indicate the issuer's ability to repay the loan, and higher ratings usually mean lower risk. Take the time to learn about each investment's potential returns and risks using online resources or financial news to gather information. Thoroughly researching your options allows you to make informed decisions and choose investments that match up with your goals.

Beginner's Guide to Mutual Funds and ETFs

Mutual funds and exchange-traded funds (ETFs) might sound like complex terms, but they're actually quite simple—and they can be a great way for beginners to start investing. Mutual funds work by pooling money from many investors to buy a wide range of stocks, bonds, or other assets. This means that when you invest in a mutual fund, you're buying into a collection of investments chosen by professional managers who handle all the decisions—what to buy, when to sell, and so on and so forth. This professional management can be reassuring for new investors who might not know where to start. ETFs, on the other hand, trade on stock exchanges the same as individual company stocks. You can buy a single share of an ETF and automatically become an owner of a group of companies that you couldn't afford to invest in otherwise. Both options offer a simple way to invest in a diversified portfolio without needing to pick individual stocks or bonds yourself (Majaski 2024).

One of the biggest advantages of mutual funds and ETFs is the ease they offer to beginners. Mutual funds provide professional management, which means experts are making the investment choices for you; unsurprisingly, this takes away the stress of deciding where to put your money. With a mutual fund, you benefit from the knowledge and experience of these managers—but this service often comes with higher fees compared to ETFs.

Moreover, if you decide to sell a mutual fund, it usually takes a day or two to finalize the transaction. By comparison, ETFs are usually cheaper because they are passively managed. They often track a specific index like the S&P 500 or Nasdaq, which means you invest in a broad market without paying for active management. ETFs also offer flexibility, as you can buy and sell them easily, like stocks. The low cost and flexibility make ETFs an appealing choice for a lot of people who are just starting out.

Choosing the right mutual fund or ETF involves thinking about two key factors. The first is the fund's performance and fees. Past performance can give you an idea of how the fund has done over time. Remember, though, past performance doesn't guarantee future results. Fees are also important because they can eat into your returns, and lower fees mean more money stays in your pocket. The fund's investment strategy and holdings are the second thing to keep an eye on. Some funds focus on growth, investing in companies expected to grow quickly. Others might focus on income, investing in stable companies that pay dividends. Make sure the fund's strategy matches up with your financial goals and risk tolerance.

Index funds are one type of ETF that offers a simple and cost-effective way to invest in the market. They aim to mirror the performance of a specific market index (like the S&P 500 and Nasdaq). This means that when you invest in an index fund, you're investing in all the companies included in that index, spreading your risk across many companies and industries. Index funds are popular because they have low fees and require little maintenance; you don't need to worry about picking the next hot stock or timing the market. Instead, you benefit from the overall growth of the market over time. This passive investment strategy is based on the idea that markets tend to rise over the long term, even if there are ups and downs along the way (Fernando 2024).

Investing in mutual funds and ETFs can be a straightforward way to grow your wealth without having to study each individual company and its stock. These funds offer diversification, professional management, and the ability to invest in a wide range of assets with ease. Understanding the basics and doing your research enables you to choose the right funds to help you reach your financial goals.

Risk and Reward: Understanding Investment Dynamics

When it comes to investing, understanding the relationship between risk and reward is like knowing that while spicy food can taste amazing, it can also make your tongue burn. The risk-return tradeoff means that the potential to earn more money usually involves taking on more risk. High-risk investments can offer big rewards—but they can also lead to big losses. Investing in a new tech startup might bring high returns if the company becomes successful. If the company fails, though, you could lose your entire investment. On the other hand, low-risk investments like government bonds offer more stability, typically providing steady returns but smaller gains.

Your comfort level with these risks is known as risk tolerance. Everyone's risk tolerance is different and depends on factors like age, financial goals, and even your personality. Teens might have a higher risk tolerance because they have more time to recover from losses, while older individuals may prefer less risky options as they get closer to retirement. Assessing your risk tolerance is as simple as thinking about how you feel about losing money. There are tools and quizzes online that can help you figure out your own risk tolerance, and knowing this can guide your investment choices.

Managing investment risk is an important part of protecting your money. One effective strategy is diversification—basically, not putting all your eggs in one basket. By spreading your investments across different assets like stocks, bonds, and real estate, you reduce the risk of losing everything if one investment fails. Asset allocation also plays a role in balancing risk and reward. This means deciding how much of your portfolio to invest in each type of asset; you might choose to invest 60 percent in stocks, 30 percent in bonds, and 10 percent in cash equivalents like money market accounts, for example. This mix can change if your risk tolerance or financial goals shift. The goal is to create a balance that feels right for you personally.

Investing is a bit like playing a sport in that you need to understand the rules and practice your skills to succeed. The same goes for managing risk and reward. Knowing your risk tolerance, diversifying your investments, and balancing your asset allocation allows you to build a portfolio that matches your goals. Calculated risks can lead to exciting opportunities, but always be sure to keep a steady foundation with stable investments. That way, you can enjoy the thrill of investing while still keeping your money safe.

Sustainable Investing: Matching Investments with Values

For a lot of us, it's not enough to simply be able to make money; what matters is doing it while supporting the causes we care about. That's the idea behind sustainable investing: putting your money into companies that match up with your values and make the world a better place. This approach uses ESG criteria, which stands for Environmental, Social, and Governance. These criteria help investors evaluate how companies perform in areas like environmental protection, social responsibility, and ethical leadership—hence the acronym. Socially responsible investing has grown a lot because people want their investments to reflect their beliefs, allowing them to support businesses that do good while potentially earning a profit (Peterdy n.d.).

Sustainable investing can benefit both the planet and your wallet. When you invest in companies that care about the environment or social issues, you contribute to positive changes. Some companies focus on reducing pollution or improving workers' rights, which can lead to healthier communities and a cleaner planet. At the same time, sustainable investments can still offer good financial returns, as companies that care about sustainability often perform well because they focus on long-term growth and risk management. Investing in these companies might help you grow your wealth while also supporting ethical practices. It can be a win-win situation that makes you feel good about where your money goes.

Finding sustainable investment opportunities does require some research. Take a look into a company's practices; do they have policies to reduce waste or protect human rights? Check their ESG ratings and scores to see how well they meet these criteria. These ratings can help you compare companies and decide which ones are a good fit for your values. You can also think about investing in green bonds, which fund projects that benefit the environment, or sustainable funds, which focus on ethical companies. Choosing investments that match your beliefs enables you to use your money to support causes you care about.

Companies leading in sustainable practices often become role models for others to follow. Some businesses have committed to using only renewable energy in their operations, while others prioritize fair trade or community development. These companies often see success from consumers and investors supporting their efforts. Choosing to invest in such companies makes you part of a movement that values ethical behavior and positive change. Investors committed to ethical investing often talk about the satisfaction that comes from knowing their money helps make the world a better place.

Sustainable investing offers a way to grow your wealth while still staying true to your values. It connects your financial goals with the bigger picture, allowing you to make a positive difference. As more people embrace sustainable investing, its impact continues to grow. Your choices matter, and you have the power to shape the future with your investments.

Chapter 7

Advanced Financial Concepts Simplified

To this point, we've done a deep dive into concepts like budgeting, investing, credit, and savings. Unfortunately, there's more you need to understand if you're going to get the most out of your money over the long term. We've touched on some of these in earlier chapters, but it's time to dig deeper into all of them.

Secret #8: Invest wisely and plan for retirement.

How Compound Interest Is Different from Regular Interest

Let's start with compound interest. Simple interest is easy enough to understand; it's only earned on the original amount. If you have $100 and a 5 percent interest rate, you'd get $5 each year, as that $100 was the original amount. With compound interest, though, you also earn interest on the $5 you earned—so the next year, you're earning interest on $105, and so on. As you can guess, earning more based on having more makes your money grow much faster. Over ten years, that same $100, with a 5 percent compound interest rate, becomes about $162. Remember Einstein's quote earlier, and it's easy to understand how compound interest is a powerful concept that's key to growing wealth over time.

Starting to save or invest early can significantly boost the benefits of compound interest. Look at two friends: One starts investing at age fifteen, and the other waits until age twenty-five. Both invest the same amount annually at the same interest rate. By the time they both reach sixty-five, the one who started at fifteen will have accumulated much more wealth than the one who started later. That ten-year head start allows compound interest more time to work its magic.

So, how do you use compound interest? One good idea is to set up automatic savings so money goes into your account regularly. Look for savings accounts that offer compound interest; even small amounts saved over a long period of time can make a big difference.

Try using an online compound interest calculator for a demonstration of how it works. Input different amounts you might save each month and see how they grow over time with compound interest. Adjust the interest rate and time period to see different outcomes. This can both help you plan and show you how starting early and contributing regularly can boost your savings. It's a great way to visualize your potential financial future.

Inflation and Its Impact: What Every Teen Should Know

Have you ever noticed that the price of your favorite snack has suddenly doubled? Or is the price the same, but now the bag is notably smaller? You used to get four Oreos, but now the package only has three. That's a small glimpse of inflation and shrinkflation in action. Roughly defined, inflation is when the overall level of prices for goods and services rises over time. In turn, this means each dollar buys less than it used to. This change heavily affects your purchasing power, which means how much you can buy with a given amount of money.

The tendency of companies to cut corners by reducing the amount of goods in a package without reducing its price, meanwhile, is a subset of inflation known as "shrinkflation." The idea is that customers will immediately spot a change in price but won't notice if the package just gets a little bit smaller. Its official term is "package downsizing," but shrinkflation is way catchier (Liberto 2024).

Inflation happens for several reasons. Sometimes, there's more demand for goods than supply, a situation known as demand-pull inflation. Other times, costs for producing goods—most commonly labor or raw materials—go up. This is called cost-push inflation. Both scenarios cause prices to be higher, impacting everything from groceries to rents to electronic gadgets.

All forms of inflation affect everyday life in all sorts of ways. Think about how a loaf of bread cost much less ten years ago than it does now. Historical examples show how inflation has changed prices over time. In the 1970s, the US experienced high inflation, which made everyday items much more expensive. People had to adjust their budgets significantly just to get by and were consequently able to afford fewer wants in order to be able to pay for their needs (Kramer 2025).

Inflation works much the same today. It's been particularly bad lately, as the post-COVID years of 2021 and 2022 saw significantly higher inflation than at any point since 1990 (Srinivasan 2025). This decrease in purchasing power means you have to spend more to maintain the same lifestyle—like trying to fill a bucket with water when the bucket keeps getting bigger. Unfortunately, inflation is a fact of life, and whether it's 2 percent or 10 percent annually, you need a plan to deal with it.

Understanding inflation is an important part of financial planning. When you save money, inflation can eat away at its value over time. Putting your money under a mattress has the same effect as making your roof out of sugar. Over time your roof disappears and your money is worth less than when you started. If your savings grow at a lower rate than inflation, you're actually losing money in terms of what you can buy. This is why it's extremely important to adjust your savings goals to account for inflation. If you plan to save $1,000 for a future purchase, think about the fact that you might need more than that amount to buy the same item in the future. Inflation also affects fixed-income investments like bonds. If inflation rises faster than the interest you receive on these investments, the real value of your returns decreases, meaning the money you earn from these investments might not keep up with rising costs.

There are a few strategies to protect against inflation. One option is to invest in inflation-protected securities like Treasury Inflation-Protected Securities (TIPS) in the US. These investments are designed to increase in value with inflation, helping your money retain its purchasing power (Chen 2024b). TIPS bonds are more attractive for retirees while younger investors may want to take advantage of growth stocks. Another strategy is one we went into in Chapter 6: diversification. Spread your investments across different asset types that tend to perform well during inflation, such as real estate and stocks. Diversifying allows you to reduce the risk of losing purchasing power, which is an effective backup plan in case one type of investment doesn't do well in high inflationary times.

Being aware of inflation and its impacts can make a big difference in how you manage your money. Being ready helps you make smarter decisions about saving and investing and makes sure that your money holds as much of its value as possible over time. While inflation is a natural and unavoidable part of the economy, understanding it and planning for it can help you stay ahead. Keep an eye on inflation trends and adjust your financial plans accordingly; by doing so, you can protect your purchasing power and maintain your financial well-being.

Taxes for Teens: Demystifying the Basics

Taxes are a part of life, whether you are young or old; there's a reason the Ben Franklin quote is famous that says: "In this world, nothing is certain except death and taxes" (NCC Staff 2023). They're basically a membership fee we all pay to keep our communities running smoothly. Picture living in a city where the roads are undrivable because there's no money to fix them, parks fall into neglected disrepair, and schools can't operate. This is what a world without taxes looks like. While people often complain about taxes, society could not function without them.

In addition to things like public schools and the maintenance of public utilities like parks and roads, taxes also cover the costs of first responders like fire departments and police. They also pay for the operation of any state, local, or national government agency, meaning they're how the post office works and how seniors get their Social Security checks. While you don't have to worry about these things as a teen, it's important to instill an understanding of taxes while you're young, and the most relevant types of taxes are income tax and sales tax. State and Federal

Income tax is what you pay to the government based on the money you earn. It's taken out in two ways: from most paychecks and yearly during tax filing. When you hear about "tax season" every year and "filing your taxes," that's referring to income tax. April 15 is the annual deadline for filing and paying income taxes. State and local sales tax, on the other hand, is added to the price of everything you buy, like clothes or snacks. Every time you buy something, you contribute a small amount to this tax.

When you start earning money, you'll notice there are payroll deductions which are the difference between what you make and what you actually take home; this is the amount taken out of your paycheck for taxes and other things like insurance plans. The amount you earn before taxes is called "gross income," in contrast to the amount after taxes are taken out, which is called "net income." This difference is due to these deductions.

Deductions on your paycheck for state and federal income taxes that are withheld and paid to the state and federal government to be applied against your next tax bill, as well as Social Security and insurance contributions. Deductions on the state and federal tax returns you file are amounts subtracted from your gross income to determine the amount of your taxable income; they can include things like mortgage or student loan interest or even a portion of your medical expenses.

Tax credits, meanwhile, work a bit differently and are thankfully easier to understand. These directly reduce the amount of tax you owe. If you owe $500 in taxes and you have a $100 tax credit, you'll only pay $400—simple enough, right? Understanding deductions and credits is a big key to smart financial planning. You may get a tax credit for purchasing an electric vehicle or improving the energy efficiency of windows or appliances in your home.

Filing taxes for the first time might seem intimidating, but it doesn't have to be. You'll need to gather all the necessary documents—if you have a steady job, you'll likely need a W-2 form from your employer. This form shows how much you earned and how much was already withheld for taxes. If you did any freelance work or gigs amounting to more than $600 in a calendar year, you'll likely be dealing with a 1099-MISC form showing miscellaneous income paid to you and reported to the IRS. This is much the same, except for the key difference that taxes are typically not taken out of payment for freelance work when you receive the money; instead, you owe them at tax time.

Once you have these documents, you can use tax filing software to get everything ironed out. Do a Google search for tax filing software like IRS FreeFile, TurboTax, H&R Block, FreeTaxUSA, and others. These programs guide you through the process step-by-step, asking simple questions and helping you fill out the forms. Many people find this type of software helpful because it makes the process easier and less stressful. It's kind of like having a tax expert right on your computer.

Staying on top of your taxes is important because if you don't file your taxes on time, you might face penalties, including fines or even interest on the taxes you owe. It's like forgetting to return a library book and then having to pay late fees. The best way to avoid this is to make sure you know the filing deadlines and plan ahead. Keeping accurate records is important, too, so save all your tax documents for deductions or credits in one place. You might need them if you get audited or if you want to check something later. Making yourself a tax file and organizing these papers can save you a lot of time and trouble in the long run.

Understanding taxes is an important step toward financial independence. They might seem complicated at first, but once you get the hang of it, filing taxes becomes just another part of adult life. Knowing how taxes work and how they impact your earnings also helps you make better decisions about your money and prepares you for more complex financial situations as you grow older. Taxes may sometimes feel like an unfair burden, but there's a reason for them. They're ultimately a way to contribute to the community and make sure that public services continue to function well for everyone. And, hey, when we call 911 we certainly want someone at the other end to pick up the phone, right?

Insurance Essentials: Protecting What Matters

Secret #9: Protect your assets.

Insurance is basically a safety net for your finances, a way to protect against unexpected losses and manage risks. You pay a small amount regularly to a company in what's referred to as an "insurance premium." If something bad happens, like an accident or getting sick, they help pay for it. Though there are a lot more types than this, the two you're likely most familiar with are health insurance and home/auto insurance. These are pretty easy to grasp; health insurance helps with medical bills, while home/auto insurance helps if your house is damaged or you're in a car accident. The idea is to protect you from having to pay huge amounts of money all at once. Things like homeowner's and renter's insurance are also designed to help people rebuild after catastrophic events like fires and other natural disasters.

When choosing insurance, think about what assets you need covered. Compare different companies, plans, and premiums. An amount known as a deductible is your portion or the amount *you have to* pay before insurance even starts to kick in in the first place; as a result, a plan with low costs but a high deductible might not be saving you much (if any) money. A coverage limit, meanwhile, tells you the limit to what insurance will pay, typically over the course of a year or lifetime.

You can also "self-insure" by saving money. This is good for smaller things, but it's less likely to be helpful in the case of big problems. We've talked about emergency funds, and those are a good example of this principle. An emergency fund is a form of self-insurance. In general, it's a good idea to have both insurance and an emergency fund in order to protect yourself.

Chapter 8

Financial Technology and Innovations

Technology is a wondrous thing when you really think about it. Previous generations would never have imagined being able to manage their money from a smartphone, no matter where they were. Today, though? That's something we can all do. No more waiting in line at the bank or trying to remember where you put your checkbook; in the current age, most people don't even know what a checkbook is.

This is the new world of financial technology, or FinTech, which has radically altered how we handle money. FinTech companies are making banking and financial services more accessible and user-friendly than ever before. Even for teens, these innovations mean gaining control over finances in ways your parents could only dream of when they were your age.

The Financial Technology Revolution

One of the biggest changes comes from companies like PayPal, Square, Venmo, and Zelle. You've probably used or at least seen some of these in action before. Venmo is designed to let you transfer money to friends, while PayPal does the same but with the added functionality of allowing you to pay retailers for things online with or without a credit card. Square helps small businesses accept payments securely using just a smartphone. Zelle links directly to your bank account and allows you to make large transfers from one account to another, making it a great tool for transactions like paying rent each month. What all of these services have in common is they make it easy to send and receive money quickly—a great thing for those of us who want to split a pizza with friends or pay someone back for movie tickets, in the moment and without having to carry cash. FinTech companies like these have created tools that make handling money as simple as sending a text.

Mobile banking apps are another huge part of the FinTech revolution. Most large banks have apps that let you check your balance, transfer money, and even deposit checks just by taking a picture. This kind of access is empowering, especially for teens who are just starting to manage their own money. If you can get to your account from anywhere at any time, you don't have to wait for a monthly statement to know how much you have spent or what you have left to spend. It's like having a digital wallet that you can use anywhere.

FinTech is not just for those who already have bank accounts, either; it's also opening doors for people who may have been left out of traditional banking. In previous generations, if you lived in a place where there weren't any banks nearby or were part of a family that didn't have a bank account, you were out of luck.

FinTech companies, however, offer solutions to these problems like micro-loans and digital wallets. These tools help people access financial services that were out of reach before. For teens, this means more opportunities to learn about money and start saving at an earlier age. The ultimate effect is to help level the playing field, ideally enabling everyone to participate in the financial system.

All these benefits do come with some challenges and risks, though. Digital transactions mean sharing personal information online, which can make your data a tempting target for hackers. It's important to use strong passwords and enable security features like two-factor authentication to secure your accounts.

FinTech companies also face regulatory challenges, as laws don't always keep up with new technology in helping to protect consumers. These companies have to deal with a complex web of rules that is often outdated and doesn't do much to actually protect the public. Don't get me wrong, regulation is important—it's just that FinTech doesn't really match up well with existing regulatory frameworks (Moss 2022). Despite these hurdles, though, FinTech continues to grow and change how we interact with money.

FinTech is reshaping the world of finance, making it more accessible, inclusive, and convenient for everyone. As these technologies continue to grow and change, they're likely to open up even more possibilities for managing money in ways we can't yet envision. Keeping a curious and informed mindset will help you make the most of these tools while staying safe and secure.

AI Assistance: Smart Tools for Money Management

Would you like to have a personal assistant who knows your spending habits better than you do? That's what Large Language Models (LLMs), and generative AI, are bringing to personal finance. LLMs are not true AI in that they aren't sentient, but they're essentially a type of advanced autocomplete that uses deep learning to make predictions—in this case, about financial matters (Kerner n.d.). All told, they're certainly changing how we manage money by integrating smart technology into financial tools.

You might have heard of AI-powered budgeting apps like Monarch, Cleo, and Digit. These apps use LLMs to analyze your spending patterns and give you personalized tips on how to save more money. Monarch excels in offering a highly customizable budgeting experience, while Cleo might send you a message saying, "Hey, you spent more on eating out last month. How about a challenge to cut back this month?" Digit, on the other hand, can automatically move small amounts of money from your checking account to your savings without you even noticing—a process that makes saving almost effortless. You can do a Google search for the highest-rated or most popular budgeting apps to compare their differences and choose the app that most closely matches your personal needs to help track spending, create budgets, and get personalized financial advice.

Virtual financial advisors are another exciting use of AI in finance. Would you like to get financial advice at any time without having to book an appointment or wait in line? Apps like Acorns and Wealthfront can do just that, providing personalized advice based on your financial goals. They analyze your income, spending, and savings to suggest strategies tailored just for you. Their greatest benefit is the ability to help you with setting goals, planning for big expenses, or figuring out the best way to pay off debt. This kind of advice used to be only available to people with lots of money, but generative AI is making it accessible to everyone.

One of the coolest things about using generative AI tools is how they make financial decisions easier and faster. The thing LLMs are really, really good at is sorting through vast amounts of data quickly and efficiently—a quality that makes them ideal for tasks like sorting through your expenses and showing you where you can cut back. It can also look at your spending and find patterns you might not notice. You might not realize, for instance, that you're spending a lot on specialty drinks or snacks each month. Even once a week, $7 spent on a fancy coffee drink adds up to $28 of your hard-earned money per month. An AI app can point this out and help you see the best ways to cut back.

Generative AI also uses automated savings algorithms to optimize how much you save, allowing that data analysis to show you when you can save a little more and prompt you to adjust accordingly. This makes saving feel less like a chore and more like a natural part of your life.

Despite the many benefits of AI in personal finance, there are some concerns to keep in mind. Generative AI doesn't generally run into things like copyright or intellectual property issues with financial applications the way it does with attempts to replace creatives, so you don't have to worry about that here (Appel, Neelbauer, and Schweidel 2023). There are still some significant concerns, though. Data privacy is a big one; when you use AI tools, you share a lot of personal information, which means your data could be at risk if the app doesn't have strong security measures.

Varying quality is another problem, as some generative AI models will be better than others—as in the famous case of Google's AI telling users to put Elmer's glue in their pizza to help the cheese stick (Robison 2024). As such, it's important to make sure the AI model you're basing your decisions off of is one of the better ones. It's important to remember that LLMs and generative AI in general are tools you can use to make certain tasks easier but you always want to double check any advice or information before relying on it completely without verification.

It's also important to be aware of inherent bias in generative AI. AI systems learn from data, and if the data is biased, the advice could be, too. This means you should always double-check the suggestions AI gives you to make sure they make sense for your situation. Another potential downside is becoming too dependent on technology for financial decisions. It's easy to rely on AI to do all the work, but it's still important to understand the reasoning behind the recommendations to make informed decisions when using generative AI to manage your finances.

Choosing the right AI tools for your needs (and for quality generally) requires a bit of research. Look at user reviews to see if the app is user-friendly and reliable; you want an app that not only works well but is easy to navigate and doesn't require a lot of effort to use. Transparency is also extremely important, so find out how the app uses your data and what security measures it has in place. Make sure the app matches your personal financial goals and habits. If you're focused on saving, choose an app that emphasizes savings strategies. If you're looking to cut back on spending, find one that offers detailed spending analysis. Most apps will have a free version or a free trial so you can try it and see how it fits your needs.

Cryptocurrency 101: What Teens Need to Know

Secret #10: Seek professional guidance when given the opportunity.

Cryptocurrency might sound like something out of a science fiction movie, but it's very real—and becoming more popular every day. At its core, cryptocurrency is a type of digital or virtual money that only exists online, meaning that, unlike the cash in your wallet, you can't touch or see it. One of the most interesting things about cryptocurrency is the technology that makes it work: the blockchain. The blockchain is basically a digital ledger or record book that keeps track of all transactions made with cryptocurrencies. It's decentralized, meaning no single person or organization controls it. This theoretically makes it secure and transparent, as everyone can see the transactions but no one can easily change them. Different countries have varying levels of cryptocurrency regulation, with some countries having more stringent rules than others.

When people talk about cryptocurrency, they often mention Bitcoin. Bitcoin was the first cryptocurrency and remains the most famous, starting back in 2009 and paving the way for many others. Ethereum is another big name in the crypto world; while Bitcoin is primarily used as digital money, Ethereum offers something called smart contracts. These are like regular contracts but digital, allowing people to create agreements that automatically execute when conditions are met. As well as Bitcoin and Ethereum, there are many other cryptocurrencies also known as altcoins. Each has its unique features and uses; some are designed for faster transactions, while others focus on privacy. Cryptocurrencies aren't just for buying things online, either.

They're also used in gaming, investing, and even supporting artists through digital art sales.

However, investing in cryptocurrencies can be very risky. One major reason is their high volatility; their prices can change dramatically in a short time. Picture buying a phone for $200 today, then tomorrow it's worth $500, then the next day it's only worth $15. That might seem extreme, but it's a pretty accurate representation of how unpredictable cryptocurrency prices can be. This makes them as nerve-racking as they are exciting. Security is another concern; cryptocurrencies are mostly stored in digital wallets, and if someone hacks into your wallet, you could lose everything with absolutely no recourse. There are also scams out there where people pretend to offer great deals only to steal your money. Being cautious and informed is key when dealing with cryptocurrencies. Cryptocurrency regulations change rapidly in the US, so make sure you're up to date on the latest laws and rules in place (Kumar 2025).

For those curious about exploring cryptocurrencies, taking small steps is wise. Always use reputable exchanges and wallets. These are platforms where you can buy, sell, and store your digital currency—essentially a bank account for your crypto. Look for exchanges with both good reviews and strong security features like two-factor authentication. Don't jump in with both feet first; get started with small investments. This allows you to learn how the market works without risking too much money. Keep up with new regulations and their impact on the valuation of cryptocurrencies, and learn as much as you can about the different types of cryptocurrencies available and their various track records. It's also always a good idea to ask adults you trust who might know more about cryptocurrency before making any big decisions. As you become more comfortable and knowledgeable, you can decide if you want to invest more.

There's a lot to learn about cryptocurrencies, particularly since the field is constantly changing. New coins and technologies are always emerging, which can be exciting and overwhelming in equal measure. Staying informed is mandatory if you're going to dip your toe into this relatively new and unregulated asset class, so read articles, watch videos, and keep up with the latest news. More than anything else, always remember to think critically and get your information from trusted sources. Not everything you read on the internet will be accurate, and there are people who might want to take advantage of newcomers. Trust your instincts and take your time—there is no need to rush into anything.

Digital Security: Protecting Your Financial Information

The downside of the Information Age is that your personal and financial information is more vulnerable than ever. Every time you use your phone or computer, you leave behind traces of your identity and financial details. Digital security is so important because common threats like identity theft and phishing scams are everywhere. Hackers use these tactics to trick people into giving away their private information. Once they have it, they can steal money—or even steal your identity and pretend to be you for purposes of fraud. Cyberattacks targeting financial data are also becoming more frequent over time. These attacks can happen to anyone, not just big companies—a fact that makes it even more important for you to make every effort to protect yourself and your information.

Luckily, there are simple steps you can take to improve your digital security. Just like we talked about with digital transactions, using strong, unique passwords for all your accounts and updating them on a regular basis is important here, as is two-factor authentication, which requires a code sent to your phone confirming it's really you before you log in. Regularly update your software and apps to patch vulnerabilities, as updates often include security fixes that protect against new threats. Staying up to date helps keep your devices safe.

Secure financial practices can also help you maintain digital security. One important habit is monitoring your bank and credit card statements for unauthorized transactions. Check them regularly to catch any suspicious activity early, and if you notice something strange, contact your credit card issuer or bank immediately. Be cautious with sharing personal information online, too; think twice before posting any personal details like your address, birthdate, or phone number on social media, as hackers can use this information to steal your identity.

Once something is online, it's hard to take back. Protecting your privacy is a key part of staying safe online, and when you post details about your upcoming vacation on social media sites, you're sending an open invitation to scammers and thieves to take advantage of your distraction from your online security. Always make sure you're set up for alerts for bank and credit card transactions so you can quickly identify fraudulent activity.

There are also tools that can help you improve your digital security. Password managers are a great resource for storing your login information securely; highly rated password managers like NordPass, RoboForm, ProtonPass, Dashlane, and 1Password all have different specifications. What they have in common is they can all generate strong passwords and remember them for you. This way, you only need to remember one master password to get into the manager. Security-focused browser extensions, meanwhile, can block tracking and keep your browsing private. These extensions prevent websites from collecting your data without your permission. They also help protect you from malicious sites that might try to steal your information. In general, using these tools can make a big difference in keeping your data safe.

Staying secure online is an ongoing process; cyber threats are always changing, so it's important to stay informed and adapt. Practice good security habits and use the tools available to you to make the most of them. Being proactive about digital security also gives you peace of mind, as knowing you're taking steps to safeguard your data allows you to focus on what really matters.

Chapter 9

Developing Healthy Financial Habits

Routines often get a bad rap. At their best, they help you start your day and manage your time, keeping you in a rhythm that makes your days run smoothly. You might have a morning routine that you follow like clockwork; washing your face, brushing your teeth, getting dressed, and having breakfast.

While we think of routines as habits like these, managing your money could be just as much a part of your daily existence as any of them. What's more, creating a financial routine can make a huge difference in your life. It's kind of like a fitness routine for your money habits; just as regular exercise keeps you fit, consistent financial habits keep your finances healthy. When you set a schedule for reviewing your budget and regularly contribute to your savings, you create a rhythm that helps you stay on track. Over time, these habits become second nature, and you'll find yourself handling money matters with ease. Now, let's talk about how to make that vision a reality.

The Importance of Consistency

Setting a fixed schedule for budget reviews is a practical first step, so choose a specific day each week or month to look over your money situation. This regular check-in allows you to see where your money is going and make any necessary adjustments. Dedicating time to this task enables you to be aware of your spending habits, allowing you to catch any issues early on. If you notice you're spending too much on eating out, you can adjust before it becomes a problem. Regularly contributing to your savings account is another important habit. It's a good idea to decide on a set amount to save each week or month, even if the minimum is just a few dollars. This consistent saving builds a safety net for future needs or emergencies.

I can't stress this enough: The most important part of this entire process is consistency. Developing consistent habits might not happen overnight, but with the right strategies, it's definitely achievable. Calendar reminders for financial tasks are a good way to stay on track, so set alerts on your phone to remind you of your budget review day or when it's time to transfer money to savings. You can also make use of structures like automatic transfers to make the process even easier. Nudges like these keep you from forgetting important tasks. Creating a financial checklist can also help you stay organized. List out your financial goals, tasks, and deadlines, then check off each item as you complete it. This visual reminder keeps you focused and motivated. It can even be a good idea to look at things you've already done, write them down, and check them off the list. You'd be surprised how much of a serotonin boost that can give you.

One hurdle you're likely to face at some point is procrastination, as it's easy to put off financial tasks, especially if they seem boring or overwhelming. Identifying personal obstacles like procrastination is the first step; acknowledge what holds you back, whether it's fear of making mistakes or simply not knowing where to start. Once you know your obstacles, you can deal with them. You can even set rewards to help you stay motivated. Promise yourself a small treat after completing a financial task; this reward system makes the process more enjoyable and gives you something to look forward to.

Technology can play a huge role in nurturing consistency. Budgeting apps with automated reminders are great for this, as they can track your spending, alert you to upcoming bills, and even offer tips to improve your financial health. Apps like GoHenry and Gimi are popular among teens for their user-friendly features. GoHenry offers a debit card and app where you can set savings goals and track spending, while Gimi helps you manage pocket money and teaches finance basics. These tools put financial management at your fingertips, which makes it a lot easier to stay consistent. Online platforms that track and visualize financial goals offer another layer of support by providing charts and graphs that show your progress over time.

Integrating these small steps and strategies into your life can give you the boost you need to overcome barriers and build a consistent financial routine that works for you. Practicing these habits will make them a part of your daily life, helping you achieve your financial goals with confidence.

Mindful Spending: Making Conscious Financial Choices

"Mindful spending" may sound like a fancy concept, but it's actually pretty simple: It just means being intentional with your money. Let's say you're at the mall, and you spot a cool pair of shoes that call out to you, tempting you to spend your hard-earned cash. Before you reach for your wallet, pause and think: Do you really need those shoes, or is this a spur-of-the-moment desire?

Allowing yourself this moment to really think before you make decisions is what mindful spending is all about. You want to make day-to-day choices that match up with your long-term goals and values rather than giving in to every impulse. Granted, maybe it actually *is* a good idea to buy that pair of shoes; the point is for you to think about the decision before you make it and figure out whether it's the best choice. When you really look at the necessity of each purchase, you start to see a bigger picture and gain the capacity to weigh your immediate satisfaction against the long-term impact on your savings. This approach helps you become more aware of how you spend your money, which naturally helps lead to better financial well-being.

One good way to practice mindful spending is to implement a thirty-day rule for major purchases. When you want to buy something expensive, wait for thirty days before making the purchase. During that time, think about whether you really need the item and how it fits into your budget. Can you earn more so you can afford this item? Will it really impact your life in a positive way? Often, you'll find that the initial urge fades, allowing you to save that money for something more important. Another useful tool is keeping a spending diary. Write down everything you buy, along with your feelings at the time of purchase. Maybe you bought a snack because you were bored or a new gadget because everyone else in your group did rather than because either of those things actually helped you. Tracking your emotional spending triggers can give you important knowledge of your habits. You can then adjust your behavior to make more deliberate choices.

Mindful spending offers numerous benefits for both your financial and personal health. As you become more intentional with your spending, you'll likely notice an increase in your savings—a pretty worthwhile goal, considering that's pretty much of the entire point of this book. You'll also experience reduced financial stress, as being in control of your spending makes you a lot less likely to worry about running out of money or regretting your impulse buys. It enables you to make decisions with confidence, knowing they line up with your priorities. This sense of control extends to other areas of your life, too, boosting your overall well-being and happiness. At its best, mindful spending creates a positive cycle where smart decisions lead to greater financial security and peace of mind.

Mindful spending isn't simply cutting costs; what it really means is making choices that support your goals and values. As you practice these techniques, you'll find that you start to spend less on things you don't need and more on what truly enriches your life. You'll gain a deeper understanding of your financial habits and develop a more broadly healthy relationship with money. Whether you're saving for college, a new phone, or simply building a safety net, mindful spending empowers you to take control of your financial future and live a life that reflects who you want to be.

Matching Your Spending with Your Values

Take a moment to think about your recent purchases. Write down three items you bought and think about why you bought them. Are they in line with your priorities? If not, think about how you can adjust your spending to better reflect what truly matters to you. This will help you make more conscious financial choices in the future.

Financial Journaling: Tracking Progress and Growth

We briefly touched on how journaling can help you earlier in this book, but it can actually make a much bigger difference than we've talked about so far. A financial journal records both financial activity and your feelings about each transaction. It's like having a personal logbook that helps you see where your money went and how you can make it work better for you in the future. Writing down your financial activities lets you spot patterns that might've escaped your notice. Maybe you spend more on weekends or spend more money on snacks when you're stressed. These patterns tell a story about your spending habits, and once you spot them, you can start to make mindful changes that help you save more and spend less.

The process of starting a financial journal is flexible; you can easily make it simple and done in a way that suits you best. It's important to decide on the format; some people prefer writing in a notebook, while others like using digital tools, and neither approach is wrong. Apps like Microsoft OneNote, Bear, Evernote, or Google Keep can be great for this if you decide to go the electronic route. Which one you pick doesn't matter so much as that point I keep hammering: consistency. Set aside time each week to update your journal. This doesn't have to take long, nor does it have to happen at a specific time; you can do it on a Sunday afternoon or a Wednesday evening, depending on what fits your schedule. The goal is simply to make it a regular habit to help you stay on top of your finances and make informed decisions.

As far as what you should include in your financial journal, an income and expenses breakdown is a good starting point. Note down all the money you receive, whether that's from a part-time job or allowance. Then, list your expenses. Be honest and include everything, even the small purchases that seem insignificant. Not leaving anything out will give you a clearer picture of your financial health. You also want to include your financial goals, so write down what you want to achieve and update your progress regularly. This keeps your goals in focus and lets you track how close you are to achieving them.

You should also use your journal to look back at where you've come from. What patterns do you see? Are there areas where you consistently overspend or under-save? Analyzing where you've been helps you better understand how to get where you want to go. Set new goals based on what you discover; maybe you want to challenge yourself to save an extra 10 percent each month or cut back on eating out. Regularly looking at your journal and adjusting based on what you learn keeps your financial strategies fresh and effective.

Documenting your financial story in a journal opens the door to greater self-awareness and mindful spending habits, allowing you to see your finances clearly and make adjustments that lead to growth. Whether you're saving for a big purchase or just trying to manage your daily expenses, a financial journal is a valuable tool to show you the bigger picture and empower you to take control of your financial future. As you continue to track your progress, you'll find that financial journaling becomes second nature. It's a simple yet effective way to keep your finances on track and achieve your goals.

Accountability Partners: Staying on Track Together

One important thing a lot of people don't seem to realize about getting your financial affairs in order is that you don't have to do it alone. An accountability partner can make a huge difference by providing support and motivation. When you share your goals with someone you trust, you feel more committed to achieving them. It's the same principle as having a workout buddy who pushes you to do your best, except the end result is more in your bank account rather than rockin' abs. You don't want to let your accountability partner down, and the extra encouragement they provide can make all the difference. External support can boost your confidence and help you stay on track, even when things get tough.

Choosing the right accountability partner is important, too. Look for someone who shares similar financial goals, as it's easier to stay motivated when you're both working toward the same target. Trust is important; you need to feel comfortable sharing your financial situation with whoever you pick for this. Open communication helps you both stay honest about your progress and any challenges you face, so make sure they will support you without judgment. Their role is to encourage and help you stay focused, not to criticize your choices; you want support and guidance rather than judgment.

A productive partnership does require some planning, so set regular check-ins to discuss your progress and any challenges you're facing. During these check-ins, look over what you've both achieved. Did you reach a savings goal or pay off a debt? Share the excitement with your partner to boost both of your morale and keep you motivated. These meetings are also the perfect time to discuss any setbacks, so talk about what went wrong and how you can improve. Working together enables you to create a supportive environment where you can both thrive.

Having an accountability partner is like having a cheerleader and a coach rolled into one in that they can keep you focused, motivated, and honest about your financial goals. Choosing the right person and setting up regular check-ins helps you create a system that supports your financial process. At their best, an accountability partner can make the process more enjoyable and rewarding by reminding you that you're not alone in your financial endeavors. Together, you can celebrate your successes and learn from your challenges, making financial management a team effort.

Chapter 10

Setting and Achieving Financial Goals

Close your eyes and picture yourself standing on a mountain, looking out at the vast range before you, where each peak and valley represents a dream or goal you have yet to reach. Setting financial goals is like charting a course through that terrain, guiding you toward each target with a clear map in hand. The goal is to help you turn your abstract visions into concrete actions by making use of the plan you've already worked out in advance. Setting goals gives your dreams structure and makes them achievable—much like how a map guides a traveler to their destination.

The Value of SMART Criteria

The SMART criteria can be a great tool when you're trying to set financial goals. The letters of the acronym stand for Specific, Measurable, Achievable, Relevant, and Time-bound. Instead of saying, "I want to save money," you might decide, "I will save $200 for a new bike by the end of summer." This goal is Specific because it states exactly what you want to achieve, and it's

Measurable because you can track your progress each month. It's Achievable because you've set a realistic target, and it's Relevant to your interests—and having a clear deadline makes it Time-bound. Using the SMART method helps clarify your goals, making them easier to manage and reach (CFI Team n.d.).

Creating a step-by-step action plan helps turn your SMART goals into reality by breaking down each goal into smaller tasks. If your goal is to save $200, determine how much you need to save each week. Write down each step you'll take to get there and check them off as you complete them. This keeps you organized and motivated, showing you how each small action brings you closer to your goal.

It's important to prioritize your goals, too, as not all of them are going to carry the same weight. Short-term goals like saving for prom tickets aren't going to make as big a difference in the long-term as goals like paying for college. List your goals and rank them based on urgency and importance, asking yourself, "Is this a need or a want?" Remember what we've talked about: Needs take priority, while wants can wait. Knowing the difference helps you focus on what matters most and prevents you from spreading your efforts too thin.

Tracking and managing your goals becomes easier with digital tools like Trello, Monday.com, and Basecamp for project management. Google Tasks, Any.do, OmniFocus, and Todoist are great for individual task management. These apps can help you track progress and deadlines, let you set reminders, and visualize your goals with charts and timelines. Of course, if you're not a fan of technology, you can also use a simple notebook to jot down your goals and check in on them regularly. Either way, visual tools make it easier to see where you stand and what steps you need to take next.

Flexibility is extremely important when working toward your goals. Life changes, and sometimes your goals need to change, too. Revisit your objectives list every three months to see if everything is still in line with your current situation. Has your vision board changed? Adjust timelines and strategies as needed. Should you look at other earning options? Adapt your plan without losing sight of your ultimate aim. Having flexibility allows your goals to stay relevant and achievable no matter what life throws your way.

The Power of Visualization: Seeing Your Financial Future

Earlier in this book, we talked about the power of vision boards. While vision boards are extremely helpful, they're also just one aspect of the broader category of visualization, a powerful tool that can help make your dreams come true. When you create mental images of your financial success, it can boost your motivation and focus your efforts. This technique isn't simply daydreaming; it requires you to see the details of your financial life clearly and use them to visualize your goals. Picture yourself saving the amount you need for a big purchase and think about the relief you'll feel when you're debt-free. These vivid images can strengthen your resolve to reach your goals.

Visualization has psychological benefits that go beyond just dreaming. It can increase your focus, helping you concentrate on what you need to do. When challenges arise, these mental images provide emotional reinforcement and remind you why you started and what you stand to gain. This technique can also help clarify your objectives. By visualizing the steps to your success, you can create a more detailed plan to achieve it. Visualization brings your daily actions in line with your long-term goals, guaranteeing every step you take is purposeful.

Many successful people use visualization to achieve their dreams. Famous athletes such as LeBron James often picture themselves winning before they even step onto the field (Baer 2020). This mental practice boosts their confidence and performance. Visualization isn't just a tool for adults; it works for anyone willing to invest time into imagining their best future.

Overcoming Obstacles: Resilience in Financial Planning

Let's say you're saving for a new phone, only to have your income from your part-time job hours cut unexpectedly. This sort of scenario is a common hurdle teens face, and changes in income that can throw off even the best-laid plans. Unexpected expenses can disrupt your savings, whether you're a teen or an adult. They're not the only potential obstacle, either; sometimes, a lack of motivation or support from friends and family can make you feel like giving up. After all, it's easy to lose sight of your goals when you're facing setbacks. What all of these issues have in common is that a big part of the solution is the same: building resilience.

Building resilience starts with a problem-solving mindset. When faced with a challenge, instead of feeling defeated, ask yourself, "What can I do to fix this?" Once you've got an answer, break down the solution into smaller parts and tackle each one. If your income changes, look for other ways to earn extra money or ways to achieve your goals more cheaply. Creating contingency plans can also help. If you set aside a small emergency fund to cover unexpected costs, even a little bit saved can go a long way in easing financial stress. Having a backup plan makes sure you're not caught off guard when life throws you a curveball.

Plenty of people have overcome financial hurdles. Entrepreneurs often face setbacks but find ways to turn challenges into opportunities, changing their business strategies or finding new markets. It's definitely possible to bounce back from financial mistakes by learning from them and trying again. Setbacks are not the end; they're just steps along the way to success.

Paying It Forward: Financial Knowledge for Your Community

By now, you've learned a few things about how money works. Now, picture the power of sharing what you've learned about money with others. Teaching financial skills serves to both help those around you and deepen your own understanding of money matters. If you're going to explain something effectively, you need to first understand it well yourself. Learning how to do so is a process that can clarify any lingering doubts. It also builds a community that's financially literate, which is a community where everyone benefits.

There are more ways to share your financial knowledge with others than you might realize. Consider starting a financial literacy club at school; you can meet once a week to discuss different topics like budgeting or saving and invite guest speakers to share their expertise. You could also choose to create educational content online; platforms like YouTube or TikTok are great for short videos that explain financial concepts in simple terms. Using visuals and examples that your peers will relate to will do a lot to make these videos fun and engaging. This can both spread your knowledge and build your confidence as a teacher.

Mentorship is another powerful tool. Mentoring younger peers allows you to guide them through the basics of money management. This could be through a local community center or a school program. Either way, partner with organizations that offer the opportunity to set up workshops or seminars. You could also volunteer in existing financial education initiatives like programs that focus on teaching kids how to save and budget—programs that can always use enthusiastic volunteers. Becoming a peer mentor in financial literacy programs helps others while reinforcing your own skills. When you choose to help those around you, you don't just build a solid network for your own well-being; you spread financial success to everyone and make the world a slightly better place in your own small way.

Financial Independence: Creating Your Plan for Success

Picture a life where you make choices based on what you want, not on what your wallet allows. At its core, this is what financial independence means: that you can support yourself without needing financial help from others and that you have the freedom to pursue dreams and opportunities without worrying about money. If you're going to get to this point, though, you're going to need a plan. Building a path to financial independence starts with setting clear income and savings targets. Decide how much money you need to earn and save each month to get where you want to be, then identify different ways to make money like part-time jobs or side hustles. Think about those investments we talked about that can be so helpful for growing your wealth over time. Each step you take in the planning stages brings you just a little bit closer to financial freedom.

Education and career planning play big roles in achieving independence, too. Your career path can affect how quickly you reach your financial goals, so it can be a good idea to choose a career that matches up with both your passions and financial aspirations. This doesn't mean forsaking anything that interests you in the service of pursuing the almighty dollar; instead, you're simply looking to invest in education and skills that open doors to better job opportunities that exist in your areas of focus. This might mean taking courses, attending workshops, or gaining certifications.

The common thread here is knowledge; the more skills you develop, the more options you'll have. You want to maximize your potential within your profession for a higher income and more savings—whatever that profession may be. Always keep in mind that education is an investment in yourself, which is likely to pay off in the form of both improved job satisfaction and increased financial security.

For all the reasons and using all the strategies we've talked about, determination and strategic planning make financial indcpendence possible even at a young age. Ultimately, you want to do everything possible to give yourself control over your life and your choices. You want to build a future that serves your aspirations and gets you where you want to go. As you work toward this goal, remember that every small step counts, and each decision brings you closer to the freedom and security you seek.

Reflect and Revise: Adapting Goals over Time

Keeping up with your financial goals can feel like trying to hit a moving target while blindfolded—if you don't stop and think about where you are from time to time. Regular reflection is like pausing to take a deep breath and adjust that aim in order to guarantee your goals are still in line with where you want to be. Over time, what has long seemed important might shift—or you might find easier paths to get to that same place. Whatever the outcome, the process of reflection helps keep your goals relevant and within reach. Without regular check-ins, you might miss out on chances to tweak things for better results or find smarter ways to reach your goals.

Effectively reviewing your goals means setting aside time every few months for a goal review. Don't be afraid to ask yourself, "Are my goals still working for me? Are there new things I need to aim for?" Self-assessment tools like simple checklists can help you see your progress, showing you where you stand and what might need adjusting going forward. Maybe you need to change your savings target because your part-time job changed, or maybe you've learned new skills that open up better opportunities than you previously had. The end result should always be to show you where you're succeeding and where you need to adjust.

If you do have to change your focus, you won't be the first person who had to change course to successfully adapt to your goals. Entrepreneurs often have to pivot their strategies to stay relevant in changing markets. Let's say there's a young business owner who changes their product line based on customer feedback, leading to greater success. As a teenager, you might likewise have to adjust your financial goals as your life grows and changes. Maybe you've planned to save for a car but then decide college is a better priority after you receive a scholarship. This shift would allow you to focus on a new, more urgent goal. Always remember that resilience, adaptability, flexibility, and regular reflection can lead to more satisfying and achievable goals.

Lifelong Learning: Continual Growth in Financial Literacy

The world is always changing, so it's no surprise that keeping up with financial knowledge is extremely important. Financial trends evolve, and regulations shift. To stay ahead, you have to commit to ongoing learning. Knowing how to save is a big part of this, but it's also a lot more than that. You need to understand how markets work, how new financial tools can benefit you, and how to work through complex decisions. Continuous learning improves your decision-making skills, which, in turn, helps you make better choices. This applies whether these choices mean whether or not to save for college or how you decide on the best investment for your goals.

Luckily, resources for learning about money are more accessible than ever before in human history. Online courses offer a flexible way to dive into topics like investing, budgeting, and even cryptocurrency, with websites like Khan Academy providing free lessons tailored to your pace and interests. Webinars from financial experts, meanwhile, can offer knowledge into current trends and strategies. Books and podcasts can also serve as valuable resources that provide stories and advice from those who've mastered the financial world—as long as you pick the right ones. Listening to a podcast on your way to school or reading a book before bed can enrich your understanding without feeling like a chore.

Adopting a curious mindset keeps your financial education in motion. Engage in conversations with friends or family about money matters; these discussions can spark new ideas and perspectives, as those around you might have ideas you never even thought of. Seek challenges that push your boundaries, such as taking a course on something unfamiliar or setting a new savings goal that sits outside your comfort zone. These experiences build confidence and open new paths. Seek out a good mentor who can also guide you; they can provide advice and share their story, offering lessons you might not learn on your own.

Remember that financial literacy is not a destination; it's a path you travel throughout life. Learning continuously allows you to build a foundation for your future which empowers you to make smart choices, adapt to changes, and seize opportunities. Whether you're planning your next step or exploring new interests, staying informed keeps you ready for whatever comes next.

Conclusion

We've packed a lot of information into this little book, but now it's up to you to take control of your own financial future.

You've read the 10 Secrets to improve your financial IQ. Maybe they made sense, or even sunk in a little. Maybe you thought they just sounded like common sense and no big deal. I guarantee, if you were to have a discussion with any self-made millionaire about how they would go about starting over and making their first million, they would say that as a teenager they would follow each of these secrets to a T; implement them, adhere to their lessons and learn from each experience along the way to a million dollars.

If you're happy with your financial life, just keep doin' what you're doin' and you'll keep gettin' what you got. If you want to become wealthy and avoid the stress of living paycheck to paycheck, start following the Secrets, and little by little, consistently you will be able to reach your financial goals.

Whether you're twelve or twenty plus years old, you now have the basics to set your life course for success and security.

The most important thing you've hopefully gained from this book is confidence. You now have the information you need to develop the skills and knowledge to make smart money choices. You're able to set financial goals, and you know how to achieve them. You can handle unexpected expenses while even planning for big dreams like college or starting a business.

So what's next? It's time to take action! Set one financial goal today. This could be scoping out opportunities to increase your earning power, saving for a new phone, or starting an emergency fund. Whatever it is, the important thing is for you to make a plan and stick to it.

Don't stop there, though; keep learning about money any way you can. Join a financial literacy club at school or attend a workshop in your community. Follow financial news and experts you trust. The more you learn, the more prepared you'll be for whatever life eventually throws your way.

Always remember that you're not in this alone. Share what you've learned with your friends and family and help them on their own financial paths. Together, you can build a community of financially savvy teens and adults who support and encourage each other. Additionally, I want you to know that I believe in your power to create the financial future you want. It won't always be easy, but I know you've got both the tools and the smarts to make it happen.

Picture yourself a few years from now. You're confident about money, and you have savings in the bank along with growing investments. Altogether, you're making smart choices and achieving your goals. That future is yours for the taking, so go out there and make it happen. Take control of your money and your life. You've got this!

One Last Favor

Hey there, money master-in-the-making!

If you made it all the way through this book—first off, huge congrats. But before you go out and start budgeting like a boss or investing like a young Warren Buffett, I'm asking for a quick favor that will take less than 60 seconds...

Please leave a review. Seriously, your words matter more than you know.

Sharing your experience can make a real impact—especially for other teens just like you who are trying to figure out how to handle their money smartly and confidently.

Think about it: what if your review is the reason someone else picks up this book and finally learns how to stop overspending, start saving, or even launch their first small business? That's powerful.

Just a few honest sentences about what helped you, what stood out, or why you think other teens should read this too. Your review is like passing the torch—sharing what you've learned and lighting the way for the next person who's feeling overwhelmed or unsure about money.

Your feedback is invaluable. Take a moment to drop a review on Amazon.com or wherever you got your copy. It's a small action with big ripple effects.

Thanks again for reading, learning, and growing. I'm proud of you. Keep going. Keep building. Keep thriving. **You've got this.**

Please scan the QR code!

References

Appel, Gil, Juliana Neelbauer, and David A. Schweidel. 2023. "Generative AI Has an Intellectual Property Problem." *Harvard Business Review*, April 7. Accessed on March 14, 2025. https://hbr.org/2023/04/generative-ai-has-an-intellectual-property-problem

Ayoola, Elizabeth. n.d. "Monthly 50/30/20 Budget Calculator." *Nerdwallet*. Accessed on March 12, 2025. https://www.nerdwallet.com/article/finance/nerdwallet-budget-calculator

Baer, Drake. 2020. "Use LeBron James' Simple Visualization Ritual to Get What You Want Out of the New Year." *Business Insider*, January 6. Accessed on March 16, 2025. https://www.businessinsider.com/forget-resolutions-use-lebron-james-visualization-ritual-for-success

Blokhin, Andriy. 2024. "The 4 Best Total Market Index Funds." *Investopedia*, December 7. Accessed on March 11, 2025. https://www.investopedia.com/articles/markets/101515/4-best-total-market-index-funds.asp

Bogle, John C. 2007. *The Little Book of Common Sense Investing: The Only Way to Guarantee Your Fair Share of Stock Market Returns*. John Wiley & Sons Inc.

Burnette, Margarette. 2024. "What Is a High-Yield Savings Account?" *Nerdwallet*, October 29. Accessed on March 13, 2025. https://www.nerdwallet.com/article/banking/high-interest-savings-account

CFI Team. n.d. "SMART Goals." *Corporate Finance Institute*. Accessed on March 16, 2025. https://corporatefinanceinstitute.com/resources/management/smart-goal/

Chen, James. 2024a. "Exchange-Traded Fund (ETF): How to Invest and What It Is." *Investopedia*, August 1. Accessed on March 11, 2025. https://www.investopedia.com/terms/e/etf.asp

Chen, James. 2024b. "What Are Treasury Inflation-Protected Securities (TIPS)?" *Investopedia*, June 7. Accessed on March 14, 2025. https://www.investopedia.com/terms/t/tips.asp

Christian, Rachel and Johna Strickland. 2024. "6 Financial Taboos That Can Prevent You From Building Wealth." *Bankrate*, October 28. Accessed on March 11, 2025. https://www.bankrate.com/investing/financial-taboos-that-hurt-wealth/

Davis, Chris. 2025. "Bonds vs. Stocks: A Beginner's Guide." *Nerdwallet*, February 20. Accessed on March 13, 2025. https://www.nerdwallet.com/article/investing/stocks-vs-bonds

Downie, Ryan. 2024. "This Is the 8th Wonder of the World, According to Albert

Einstein. And Utilizing It Correctly Can Help Make Saving for Retirement an Absolute Breeze." *Nasdaq*, March 16. Accessed on March 13, 2025. https://www.nasdaq.com/articles/this-is-the-8th-wonder-of-the-world-according-to-albert-einstein.-and-utilizing-it

Dweck, Carol. 2007. *Mindset: The New Psychology of Success*. Ballantine Books.

Fernando, Jason. 2024. "What Are Index Funds, and How Do They Work?" *Investopedia*, July 25. Accessed on March 13, 2025. https://www.investopedia.com/terms/i/indexfund.asp

Kagan, Julia. 2024. "Credit Rating: Definition and Importance to Investors." *Investopedia*, March 9. Accessed on March 13, 2025. https://www.investopedia.com/terms/c/creditrating.asp

Kerner, Sean Michael. n.d. "What Are Large Language Models (LLMs)?" *TechTarget*. Accessed on March 14, 2025. https://www.techtarget.com/whatis/definition/large-language-model-LLM

Klein, Andrew. n.d. "Eco-Fashion Designer." *Scholastic SuperSTEM*. Accessed on March 12, 2025. https://superstem.scholastic.com/earth-day-careers/eco-fashion-designer.html?language=english#870L

Kumar, Ananya. 2025. "What Is Next for Crypto Regulation in the US?" *Atlantic Council*, January 23. Accessed on March 14, 2025. https://www.atlanticcouncil.org/blogs/econographics/what-is-next-for-crypto-regulation-in-the-us/

Kramer, Leslie. 2025. "How the Great Inflation of the 1970s Happened." *Investopedia*, March 7. Accessed on March 14, 2025. https://www.investopedia.com/articles/economics/09/1970s-great-inflation.asp

Liberto, Daniel. 2024. "Shrinkflation: What It Is, Reasons for It, How to Spot It." *Investopedia*, August 30. Accessed on March 14, 2025. https://www.investopedia.com/terms/s/shrinkflation.asp

Little, Kendall. 2024. "Take the 52-Week Money Challenge: What It Is and How to Do It." *Bankrate*, December 19. Accessed on March 13, 2024. https://www.bankrate.com/banking/savings/52-week-savings-challenge/

Lodge, Michelle. 2024. "10 Successful Young Entrepreneurs." *Investopedia*, February 3. Accessed on March 11, 2025. https://www.investopedia.com/10-successful-young-entrepreneurs-4773310

Majaski, Christina. 2024. "ETF vs. Mutual Fund: What's the Difference?" *Investopedia*, December 12. Accessed on March 13, 2025. https://www.investopedia.com/articles/investing/110314/key-differences-between-etfs-and-mutual-funds.asp

Melinn, Cathal. 2024. "What Is SEO and How Does It Work?" *Digital Marketing Institute*, February 27. Accessed on March 12, 2025. https://digitalmarketinginstitute.com/blog/what-is-seo

Moss, Jillian. 2022. "The Regulatory Challenges of FinTech." *The Regulatory Review*, June 14. Accessed on March 14, 2025. https://www.theregreview.org/2022/06/14/moss-regulatory-challenges-of-fintech/

National Endowment for Financial Education. 2017. "Millennials Show Alarming Gap Between Financial Confidence and Knowledge." February 9. Accessed on March 11, 2025. https://www.nefe.org/news/2017/02/millennials-show-alarming-gap-between-financial-confidence-and-knowledge.aspx

NCC Staff. 2023. "Benjamin Franklin's Last Great Quote and the Constitution." *National Constitution Center*, November 13. Accessed on March 14, 2025. https://constitutioncenter.org/blog/benjamin-franklins-last-great-quote-and-the-constitution

NMAH. 2011. "Build a Better Mousetrap." *National Museum of American History*, January 26. Accessed on March 12, 2025. https://americanhistory.si.edu/explore/stories/build-better-mousetrap

Paul, Trina. 2024. "When Did Credit Scores Start? A Brief Look at the Long History Behind Credit Reporting." *CNBC*, October 31. Accessed on March 13, 2025. https://www.cnbc.com/select/when-did-credit-scores-start/

Peterdy, Kyle. n.d. "ESG (Environmental, Social, & Governance)." *Corporate Finance Institute*. Accessed on March 13, 2025. https://corporatefinanceinstitute.com/resources/esg/esg-environmental-social-governance/

Ramsey Solutions. 2024a. "Which States Require Financial Literacy for High School Students?" August 19. Accessed on March 10, 2025. https://www.ramseysolutions.com/financial-literacy/states-require-financial-literacy-in-high-school

Ramsey Solutions. 2024b. "How to Win a No-Spend Challenge." December 30. Accessed on March 13, 2025. https://www.ramseysolutions.com/budgeting/no-spend-month

Robison, Kylie. 2024. "Google Promised a Better Search Experience—Now It's Telling Us to Put Glue on Our Pizza." *The Verge*, May 23. Accessed on March 14, 2025. https://www.theverge.com/2024/5/23/24162896/google-ai-overview-hallucinations-glue-in-pizza

Rose, Dottie. 2023. "World's Youngest CEO Launches Boundary Breaking Platform." Accessed on March 11, 2025. https://dottierosefoundation.org/2023/02/worlds-youngest-ceo-launches-boundary-breaking-platform/

Segal, Troy. 2024. "What Is a Custodial Account?" *Investopedia*, November 25. Accessed on March 11, 2025. https://www.investopedia.com/terms/c/custodialaccount.asp

Shoutout Atlanta. 2023. "Meet Sara 'Saray Young | Author, Emcee & Jewelry Designer." June 14. Accessed on March 11, 2025. https://shoutoutatlanta.com/meet-sara-saray-young-author-emcee-jewelry-designer/

Srinivasan, Hiranmayi. 2025. "Historical U.S. Inflation Rate by Year: 1929 to 2025." *Investopedia*, February 2. Accessed on March 14, 2025. https://www.investopedia.com/inflation-rate-by-year-7253832

Sternlicht, Alexandra. 2020. "These Teen Sisters Cooked Bath Bombs In Their Kitchen. Now It's A $20 Million-Plus Per Year Business." *Forbes*, February 21.

Accessed on March 11, 2025. https://www.forbes.com/sites/alexandrasternlicht/2020/02/21/these-teen-sisters-cooked-bath-bombs-in-their-kitchen-now-its-a-20-million-plus-per-year-business/

The Editors of Encyclopedia Brittanica. 2025. "Dell." *Britannica Money*, March 11. Accessed on March 12, 2025. https://www.britannica.com/money/Dell-Inc

Ziv, Shahar. 2025. "Student Loan Delinquency Rate Skyrockets As 4 Million Borrowers Are Behind." *Forbes*, March 7. Accessed on March 13, 2025. https://www.forbes.com/sites/shaharziv/2025/03/07/student-loan-delinquency-rate-skyrockets-4-million-borrowers-behind/

Made in United States
North Haven, CT
04 November 2026

21769525R00076